Human-Computer Interface Design Guidelines

Human/Computer Interaction
A Series of Monographs, Edited Volumes, and Texts

SERIES EDITOR
BEN SHNEIDERMAN

Directions in Human/ Computer Interaction
Edited by Albert Badre and Ben Shneiderman

Online Communities:
A Case Study of the Office of the Future
Starr Roxanne Hiltz

Human Factors In Computer Systems
Edited by John Thomas and Michael Schneider

Human Factors and Interactive Computer Systems
Edited by Yannis Vassiliou

Advances in Human/Computer Interaction Volume One
Edited by H. Rex Hartson

Empirical Studies of Programmers
Edited by Elliot Soloway and Sitharama Iyengar

Human-Computer Interface Design Guidelines
C. Marlin "Lin" Brown

Expert Systems: The User Interface
Edited by James A. Hendler

Empirical Studies of Programmers: 1987 Workshop
Edited by Gary Olson, Elliot Soloway and Sylvia Sheppard

In preparation:

Human Factors in Management Information Systems
Edited by Jane M. Carey

Advances in Human/Computer Interaction Volume Two
Edited by H. Rex Hartson and Deborah Hix

Online Helps: Design and Implementation
Greg Kearsley

Socializing the Human/Computer Environment
Jerry J. Vaske and Charles E. Grantham

Human-Computer Interface Design Guidelines

C. Marlin "Lin" Brown
Xerox Corporation
Sunnyvale, California

Ablex Publishing Corporation
355 Chestnut Street
Norwood, New Jersey 07648

Second Printing 1989.

Copyright © 1988 by Ablex Publishing Corporation

Printed in the United States of America

Book Design and Electronic Prepress Production by
Aaron Marcus and Associates
Berkeley, California

Library of Congress Cataloging in Publication Data

Brown, C. Marlin
    Human-computer interface design guidelines

    (Human/computer interaction)
    Bibliography: p.
    Includes index.
1. Computer software- -Development- -Human Factors.
2. Computer input-output equipment. I. Title.
II Series: Human/computer interaction (Norwood, N.J.)
QA76.76.D47B76 1987   004' .01'9   87-14473
ISBN O-89391-332-4

About The Author

Dr. C. Marlin " Lin" Brown is a Senior Human InterfaceScientist for Xerox Corporation's Strategic Business Office. He is responsible for helping to shape the corporate strategy for Human Interface design of office products for the next decade. He works closely with emerging technologies at Xerox Palo Alto Research Center (PARC) to develop future product concepts and to facilitate technology transfer from the research environment into product design.

He received a Ph.D. degree from the Georgia Institute of Technology in human factors engineering psychology and has taught graduate courses in human factors and systems management for the University of Southern California.

He has developed system concepts and human-computer interface designs for a variety of systems, including a computerized mobile pulmonary lab for occupational lung screening; the computerization of Emory Hospital Pulmonary Lab in Atlanta; a Cardiac Data Base of diagnosis, surgery, and follow-up data on thousands of heart patients; large corporate data bases for finance, engineering, and materiel at Lockheed; and operating concepts and user interface designs for several space systems, including a mission control center for the Space Shuttle. He developed a design for a flexible, reconfigurable computer workstation, for which he received Lockheed's award for technical excellence.

Acknowledgements

Several groups of people played a significant role in the technical background, support, and writing of *Human-Computer Interface Design Guidelines.* Dr. John Mangelsdorf and Dr. Kenneth Siler served as my mentors and supporters when I was a fledgling in human-computer interface design. My colleagues at Lockheed and I worked closely together in formulating and refining many of the concepts I have subsequently included in this book. I'd like to specifically thank Dr. John Mangelsdorf, Homer Burkleo, Dr. Richard Olsen, Allan Williams, Deborah Brown, and Ronald Perkins.

In the process of writing the book Dr. Ben Shneiderman, the series editor, has been a valuable reviewer, advisor, and friend. Dr. Michael Burns of AT&T Bell Labs, Aaron Marcus and Associates, and Wilbert Galitz of Galitz Incorporated provided detailed reviews that contributed much to the book.

I also appreciate the support that Dr. Stuart Parsons and John Duddy gave to my work on this book at Lockheed, and the enthusiasm Dr. Robert Glass has shown at Xerox.

Table of Contents

Chapter One
General Human-Computer Interface
Concepts

Introduction

This text is a set of practical suggestions and guidelines to aid designers of the interface between computer systems and their users. These guidelines are drawn from diverse sources, including

1 evidence from experiments,

2 predictions from theories of human performance,

3 principles of cognitive psychology,

4 principles of ergonomic design, and

5 evidence gathered through engineering experience.

Many of these guidelines have developed from expert judgment, common sense, and practical experience. Experimental results on which to base user interface design recommendations are relatively scarce. Existing experimental data are often too situation-specific to provide general design guidance. User interface design decisions, however, must be made even when no relevant experimental data exist. The application of design guidelines provides a systematic approach to

1 take advantage of practical experience,

2 disseminate and incorporate applicable experimental findings,

3 incorporate rules of thumb, and

4 promote consistency among designers responsible for different parts of the system's user interface.

In some design situations, certain guidelines may be inapplicable or impractical due to hardware, software, or cost constraints. In other cases, constraints may allow the designer to observe one guideline only at the expense of violating another. This necessitates tradeoffs and priority judgments. In other cases, a guideline that is important in certain kinds of dialogues or applications may be trivial or even counterproductive in others. (Exceptions and tradeoffs are noted for many of the guidelines in this book.)

These problems are inherent in trying to use guidelines in situations unforeseen by their authors. Many readers who apply these guidelines in their own designs will probably tailor the list to fit the purposes, constraints, and users of their system. For these readers several suggestions can be offered.

1 Keep in touch with the growing body of relevant experimental data which may validate, extend, qualify, or invalidate some of the recommendations of this book.

2 Consider each guideline in light of the special requirements and constraints of your users, equipment, and development environment.

3 Employ prototyping, pilot tests, and user acceptance tests at all stages in the development of your product to evaluate and refine design concepts before they are finalized.

These guidelines should be considered neither as final nor as a panacea to guarantee the optimal user interface. However, system designs that are developed with careful consideration of these guidelines and the design philosophy they represent should result in more usable computer systems. The potential benefits to users include reduced training, reduced errors, increased efficiency, and increased user satisfaction. Design projects and their personnel can also benefit. Increased user acceptance or sales, improved productivity due to design consistency, and reduced training requirements due to consistent, documented design procedures can result.

The remainder of this chapter discusses some of the general concepts that underlie the specific guidelines to be presented in subsequent chapters. Most of the rest of the book is a listing of guidelines, often including examples to contrast observing the guideline with violating it. These examples are meant to help make the items clear and the concepts concrete. Finally, the last chapter presents a strategy for implementing human-computer interface design principles in the development of a product or project.

▄▄▄ Mental Processing Requirements

One of the most useful design philosophies for developing user-oriented human-computer interfaces considers the computer system simply as a tool to aid the user in performing tasks. This philosophy emphasizes the duty of the tool's designer to ensure that the tool simplifies, rather than complicates, the user's tasks. A tool which requires more time, effort, and training to use than the task requires without the tool is not likely to be a successful product.

In human-computer interface design, the "computer as a tool" philosophy implies that designers must actively pursue techniques to reduce the mental processing operations required just to be able to use the tool. Mental processing operations include requirements for the user to learn complex commands and syntax, memorize encrypted codes and abbreviations, or translate data into other units or formats before they can be applied to the problem at hand.

4   A well designed computer system permits use of the tools it offers without requiring users to dedicate extensive mental processing to operations inherent in the system design rather than the task. Furthermore, its tools are designed to also reduce task-specific mental processing, especially those types of processing that are performed more effectively by computers than by people, such as calculations and accurate storage and recall of large amounts of pre-specified information. Many of the techniques that have proven useful in achieving these goals are discussed in the guidelines presented in this book.

▄▄▄ Allocation of Functions

One of the most important categories of design decisions in developing effective human-computer interfaces is the allocation of functions to be performed by the user or by the computer.

In the design of an effective human-computer interface, allocating functions to be performed by either the user or the system should be based on an understanding of the capabilities and limitations of both the system and the users: The computer should do the things that computers do better and the user should do the things that people do better. Unfortunately, these decisions are often either based exclusively on hardware, software, and cost concerns, or they are made without any explicit analysis of the allocation of functions.

Allocation of functions includes decisions like the following:

1 Will the user be required to commit the commands required to perform a task to memory, or will a list of the currently available options be presented?

2 Will the user be required to perform mental arithmetic on displayed data, or will the computer system calculate and display (perhaps graphically) the data in the form required to perform the user's task?

3 Will the software keep track of previous user entries in a multiple step procedure, permitting the user to correct an error in a later step without starting the whole procedure over? Or will the user be required to return to step 1 if an error is made in step 9?

4 Will the user monitor a large table of parameter values to determine if all are within safe limits? Will the display highlight suspect parameters to draw the user's attention? Or will the software monitor all parameters automatically, diagnose patterns of values, and present conclusions and recommended actions to the user?

The human factors literature shows human capabilities and limitations that should be taken into account in allocating functions. Many human factors engineering texts show lists comparing functions that people tend to perform better and those that machines tend to perform better. These lists have been called "MABA-MABA" lists for "Men Are Better At ...; Machines Are Better At ... " (Price, 1985). Table 1 shows such a comparison, based on McCormick's (1970) text and an article by Estes (1980), which specifically contrasted human memory with computer memory.

This table must be qualified by noting that advances in technology, especially in artificial intelligence technology, are constantly expanding the list of functions that a machine can perform. In particular, artificial intelligence permits computers to be less dependent on specific, pre-programmed instructions. The technology is providing techniques that allow computers to reason from rules, benefit from experience, utilize incomplete or uncertain information, and recognize patterns effectively.

Table 1.1. Relative Capabilities of Humans and Machines

Humans Generally Better	Machines Generally Better
Sense low level stimuli	Sense stimuli outside human's range
Detect stimuli in noisy background	Count or measure physical quantities
Recognize constant patterns in varying situations	Store quantities of coded information accurately.
Sense unusual and unexpected events	Monitor pre-specified events, especially infrequent ones
	Make rapid and consistent responses to input signals
Remember principles and strategy	Recall quantities of detailed information accurately
	Process quantitative data in pre-specified ways
Retrieve pertinent details without a priori connection	
Draw upon experience & adapt decisions to situation	
Select alternatives if original approach fails	
Reason inductively: generalize from observations	Reason deductively: infer from a general principle
Act in unanticipated emergencies and novel situations	Perform repetitive pre-programmed actions reliably
	Exert great, highly controlled physical force
Apply principles to solve varied problems	
Make subjective evaluations Develop new solutions	
Concentrate on important tasks when overload occurs	Perform several tasks simultaneously
	Maintain operations under heavy information load
	Maintain performance over extended periods of time
Adapt physical response to changes in situation	

From McCormick, E.J. Human factors engineering. New York: McGraw-Hill, 1970, pp. 20-21; Estes, W.K. Is human memory obsolete? American Scientist, 1980, 68, pp. 62-69.

The implication of these comparisons for human-computer interface design is that the best role for humans is to control, monitor, serve as decision maker, and respond to unexpected events. The computer is better suited to store and recall data, process information using pre-specified procedures, and present options and supporting data to the user. Human memory is flexible, but slow, unreliable and imprecise. Computer memory is fast, reliable, and accurate, but is limited to what has been programmed.

The space shuttle program has provided numerous examples of the importance of the human role in solving unexpected problems. NASA has been able to exploit the creative problem solving abilities of astronauts and controllers to save many valuable missions and payloads that would certainly have been lost in an automated, unmanned program. Many of the anomalies that have occurred on various missions were quite unlikely and unpredictable. Without human work-arounds and jury-rigging these anomalies could not have been resolved. NASA has also recognized the appropriate allocation of functions to machines and provided computer functions to calculate, analyze, and summarize massive amounts of complex data into quantities and formats that are manageable by humans as problem solving tools. Computer simulations and decision aids permit controllers to evaluate proposed solutions before using them.

In routine interface design situations, several rules of thumb for allocation of functions seem useful:

1   Reduce the amount of memorization of commands, codes, syntax, and rules required of the user. For example, permit users to select from a list of displayed options rather than entering memorized command strings.

2   Reduce the amount of mental manipulation of data required of the user. Present data, messages, and prompts in clear and directly useable form.

3   Reduce requirements for the user to enter data. If information is available to the system, or if the design can make this information available to the system, do not require the user to enter it manually. Structure dialogues so that manual user entries are minimized. Selecting from displayed lists instead of entering choices manually is also an effective technique to reduce input requirements.

General Human - Computer
Interface Concepts

4 Provide computer aids (such as online checklists, summary displays, and online problem diagnosis) to reduce the amount of mental processing required of the user to remember and execute complex procedures with many steps.

5 Use computer algorithms to pre-process complex, multi-source data and present a composite, integrated view of complex patterns or relationships among many variables.

■ Mental Models of System Operation

Another important concept in human-computer interface design is that of mental models. A mental model is a cognitive representation or conceptualization of a system's internal mechanics developed by a user (Halasz and Moran, 1983). The user's mental model of the system's parts and their operations permits the user to predict the appropriate procedure for a desired outcome, even if he or she has forgotten the procedure or never encountered it before. A user's mental model thus provides a framework for understanding how the system works that is developed and refined when the user is learning and using the system.

The sophistication, accuracy, and usefulness of the mental models that different users will develop can vary considerably. Some users may develop models that accurately represent actual system behavior at all times, while others may develop models that are inaccurate, misleading, and error-provoking. As users build up experience using computers, they develop models that may prove effective to some degree when learning a new computer system.

The critical point for designers of human-computer interfaces, however, is that decisions made by the designer can have major impact on the ease or difficulty with which a typical user will be able to develop an effective mental model of the system. Interfaces with extensive rules and syntax, no underlying overall framework, or internally inconsistent conventions can befuddle even the most sophisticated user. Fortunately, there are several useful principles to help the designer ensure that the user interface is conducive to the development of effective user models. These principles include consistency, physical analogies, user expectations, and stimulus-response compatibility.

Consistency

Consistency is one of the most obvious human-computer interface design goals, but one that requires perhaps the most discipline in the design process. The members of a team of designers will typically have responsibility for different subsystems or pieces of the system. Often each member will also have a somewhat different concept of the optimal user interface approach. If a consistent set of conventions is not decided upon, documented, and incorporated into all subsystems, the user is likely to encounter a system that appears to have a different set of interaction rules for every transaction.

As the user is beginning to develop a mental model of how the system works, he or she may encounter a new transaction for which the model is inappropriate. In this case the user must now either

1 develop a new, more complex model, or

2 develop multiple models and try to remember which model is appropriate for which transaction.

In either case, the value of the using a mental model to avoid the necessity to rote memorize the steps required by every transaction is undermined by the memorization and mental processing required to use the model.

Consistency is important not only for specific actions, but also for classes of actions at various levels. For example, in a word processing application, consistency is not only important in the response required for deleting a character, but the responses required for deleting a character, a word, a line, and a paragraph should also be consistent with each other.

Physical Analogies

In developing a user-computer interface, designers can take advantage of the value of analogies to physical objects. Users will often rely on physical analogies to construct a mental model anyway, so the interface can exploit that tendency to develop a system that users will perceive as natural, logical, and easy to understand. For example, novices are likely to try to conceptualize a word processing program by drawing analogies to a typewriter (Douglas and Moran, 1983). The developers of the word processing program might anticipate this and design protocols and conventions to take advantage of the similarity in the way the word processor works to the way a typewriter works.

Promising recent developments in human-computer interface design include the emergence and refinement of direct manipulation dialogues. Representations of the objects of interest, often in the form of pictorial representations called icons, are manipulated directly by the user. Shneiderman (1982b) has described three characteristic features of direct manipulation:

1 The object of interest is represented continuously.

2 Physical actions or labelled button presses are used in place of complex syntax.

3 Operations are rapid, incremental, and reversible; their impact on the object of interest is immediately visible.

Many of the concepts of direct manipulation, (also referred to as visual interfaces), were developed for the Xerox STAR (Smith, Irby, Kimball, Verplank, and Harslem, 1982), and later applied in the Apple Lisa and Macintosh. (STAR is a trademark of Xerox Corporation; Lisa and Macintosh are trademarks of Apple Computer Corporation.) These systems organize the options available to the user by an office desk analogy: text files are represented by icons of pieces of paper lying on the "desktop"; floppy disks are represented by icons of disks; files can be combined into a file folder by dragging the icon for each file and laying it on top of the file folder icon; files are deleted by dragging their icons onto an icon of a wastebasket. An example is shown in Figure 1.1.

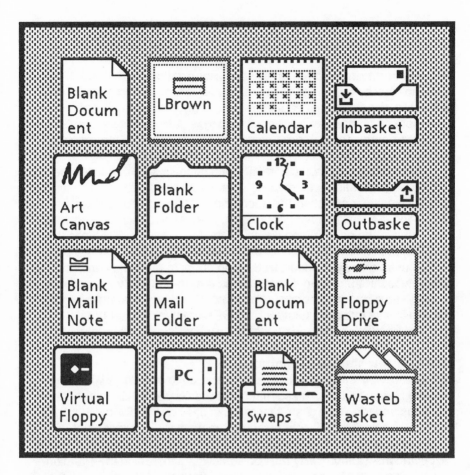

Figure 1.1
Example of the Use of Icons for Direct Manipulation

Expectations and Stereotypes

A related principle can help in designing interfaces that naturally foster effective user mental models. Interfaces can capitalize on commonly held expectations to minimize requirements to learn new and unfamiliar associations. For example, by using the color red for alarm signals, yellow for caution, and green for safe, the designer takes advantage of the traffic signal association that most users learned quite well before they ever used a computer. The need to learn an idiosyncratic code is thus eliminated, and there is one less barrier to user proficiency.

User expectations are important in human-computer interface design not only in the positive sense as a means of augmenting usability, but also in avoiding the negative effects of contradicting them. If an interface design not only fails to incorporate an existing user expectation, but also contradicts it by requiring the opposite user response from what is expected, negative transfer of learning is likely. The user will be predisposed to make an erroneous response, and may have years of prior experience to overcome before mastering the required response.

The associations that are commonly held by the relevant group of people are called population stereotypes. One must consider the particular user population when selecting the appropriate stereotype for design decisions. Specialized user populations may have unique stereotypes not found in the general population, or they may have stereotypes that are contradictory to those held in the general population. If the product will be used only by a specialized group of users, it should conform to the stereotypes of that group. In the electric power industry, for example, red usually denotes "on", "open" , or "flowing". A display system designed for use in that industry should follow that stereotype, rather than the general population stereotype that red means "stop" or "danger".

Stimulus-Response Compatibility

Stimulus-response compatibility is a term used to refer to relationships among stimuli and responses that make the connection between the stimulus and the appropriate response an easy one. McCormick (1970) has defined compatibility as the spatial, movement, or conceptual features of stimuli and of responses that are most consistent with human expectations. Compatibility may be somewhat inherent in the situation, such as pressing the right cursor control key to move the cursor to the right, or it may be learned, such as driving on the right side of the road in the United States.

Compatibility has been defined in another way that may be more valuable in providing guidance to the designer. Fitts and Seeger (1953) defined stimulus-response compatibility as the ensemble of stimulus and response combinations that results in a high rate of information transfer. Compatibility results from situations that promote rapid processing of information by the user. These situations minimize the amount of mental processing or recoding required of the human. For designers of human-computer interfaces, this definition implies that the computer should present information in a form that is consistent with the users' tasks and with the capabilities and limitations of human information processing. Functions involving translating, calculating, and recalling precise details from memory should be performed by the computer.

Compatibility also requires that the designer consider the relationship between the display design and the responses required of the user. Dialogue and display designs should ensure that the spatial, movement, and conceptual relationships among stimuli and associated responses are compatible. For example, if the current function definitions of a set of programmable function keys are to be displayed on the video screen, the arrangement of the definitions on the screen should correspond to the arrangement of the function keys on the keyboard.

Ease of Learning, Ease of Use, and Functionality

A critical step in defining the design philosophy for the user interface is to establish the appropriate balance of ease of learning, ease of use, and functionality. Ease of learning is the extent to which a novice user can become proficient in using a system with minimal training and practice. Ease of use is the extent to which the system allows a knowledgeable user to perform tasks with minimal effort (for example, less time, fewer key strokes, or fewer transactions). Functionality is the number and kind of different functions the system can perform.

Many believe that designing a system to be easy to learn requires an inevitable sacrifice in functionality and in ease of use for skilled users. If this is the case, perhaps extensive emphasis on ease of learning is short-sighted. Novices may be able to learn to use the system quickly, but may soon tire of wading through seemingly endless menus, when they really do not need the menus after the first few sessions. Furthermore, if the designers have protected users from complexity by incorporating only the most basic functions, the users may soon outgrow the system. Desirable capabilities may be missing, and failure of the system as a product may result. Designing strictly for ease of learning may result in a product that users may not consider useful, even if it is easy to learn.

Fortunately, the sacrifice of usability and functionality for ease of learning is not inevitable. Careful attention to human-computer interface design can ensure that features are provided that support all three. In fact findings by Roberts and Moran (1983) --comparing text editors -- and Whiteside, Jones, Levy, and Wixon (1985) -- comparing user interfaces -- both show that the systems that were the best for novices (easiest to learn) were also the best systems for experts (easiest to use).

General Human - Computer
Interface Concepts

Burns, Warren, and Rudisill (1986) showed that a design to aid novices can also benefit experts. They compared performance time and errors of experts and novices on existing display formats and on reformatted displays with improved grouping, better labelling, and fewer abbreviations. The experts were NASA astronauts, flight controllers, and trainers who were all highly skilled in using the existing displays. The results showed large improvements in both speed and accuracy for novices when they used the reformatted displays. The results for experts were even more interesting. Their accuracy improved and their speed was no different using the reformatted displays, in spite of the fact that they had years of experience using the existing displays and no previous experience on the reformatted displays.

Several techniques are useful in optimizing ease of learning, ease of use, and functionality. These techniques include the following, which are discussed in more detail below:

1 Design for novices, experts, and intermittent users.

2 Avoid excess functionality.

3 Provide multiple paths.

4 Design for progressive disclosure and graceful evolution.

Design for Novices, Experts, and Intermittent Users

Most systems should be designed to incorporate the needs of novices, intermittent users, and experts. (Exceptions are systems such as airline ticketing, where the required training can be assured and where the high volume of transactions places extreme emphasis on speed of operation.) Novices may need extensive prompting and rely heavily on menus. Intermittent users may require less prompting, but need to refer to menus occasionally for forgotten details or functions they have not used before. Experts have memorized the sequence of requests they use frequently, and they need not be encumbered by sequences of menus.

Experts should be able to shortcut or bypass menus and prompting when desired. They should be able to define complex sequences of actions as a higher order command or macro, such that the entire sequence can be initiated by a single user action. Menus should be available for use by novices, intermittent users, and experts as needed, but time-saving shortcuts should also be available for those who are ready to use them.

Note that in complex computer applications, there may be few users who are experts in all aspects of system usage. Most become expert over time in those functions they use frequently. However, they use other functions only intermittently, and may have never encountered some before. There is often a danger, then, in assuming that all users are experts and designing exclusively for experts.

Avoiding Excess Functionality

If the designer tries to include a command or option for every conceivable function that could be incorporated into the system, users are likely to be overwhelmed. Candidate functions should be prioritized for the estimated frequency and criticality of their use. Those functions of lowest priority should either be eliminated or made accessible through secondary paths if they would lead to clutter or confusion in the primary paths.

Providing Multiple Paths

The preceding paragraphs have hinted at this technique. It is perhaps the key for simultaneously providing ease of learning, ease of use, and appropriate functionality. Multiple path techniques include the following:

1 Menu bypass, which permits the user to request a desired option, display, or transaction directly by entering a command, code, or other identifier. The user is thus able to bypass a hierarchical menu sequence.

2 Stacking or type-ahead techniques permit the user to make the inputs that would be appropriate for a series of menus or transactions in a single entry. For example a sequence of commands could be entered with a delimiter such as a semicolon separating subsequent commands, or a memorized sequence of menu selections could be entered by typing several individual responses as a single entry.

3 User-defined macros permit the user to save a sequence of individual commands or actions (often as a file), name the sequence, and later initiate the whole series by entering only the sequence name, code, or function key.

General Human - Computer
Interface Concepts

4 Input device options permit the user to initiate a function from more than one input device. For example menu selection might be accomplished by pointing with a separate cursor control device (for example mouse, joystick), with cursor control arrow keys on the keyboard, by typing item numbers or letters, by a touch sensitive overlay, or by voice recognition device entry of item names. A given user's device of choice could vary with experience, preference, task, or operating conditions.

Design for Progressive Disclosure and Graceful Evolution
The approach used in developing multiple path designs should encourage and support the gradual evolution of a user from a novice to an expert. The fundamentals that the user has to know to perform meaningful, relevant tasks using the system should be learned easily with minimal training and experience. As he or she gains confidence and is willing to explore more, the user encounters and masters more and more of the details for fine-tuning, customizing, and streamlining the tasks performed on the system. *Shneiderman, 1986*

This approach benefits novices by not overwhelming them with the full system complexity until they have acquired the basics and some confidence in using the system. It also benefits users who are more experienced, because their interest and motivation is maintained by the discovery of new "tricks" to do things faster, easier, or with more elaborate results. Some design features that encourage graceful evolution are listed below:

1 Make fundamental functions easy to learn. Fundamental functions are those required to do anything meaningful using the system. For example, a word processing program should allow the novice user to create a simple document, save, retrieve a document, and perform basic editing functions (such as inserting, deleting, and modifying characters).

2 Make frequently used functions easy to perform. High volume interactions are the first candidates for some of the time-saving techniques mentioned in the multiple path discussion above.

3   Encourage experimentation. A system designed consistently according to an appropriate underlying user model can encourage experimentation and facilitate graceful evolution. The user can extrapolate from the way familiar functions work to guess with reasonable confidence about how an unfamiliar function works.

4   Minimize the consequences of error through reversible actions. This also encourages experimentation and graceful evolution. The capability to quickly recover from any action is critical to encouraging exploration and building users' confidence. For each simple action provide an UNDO, RESTORE, or inverse function. For critical functions or those that may result in data loss or irreversible changes, display a message warning of the irreversible nature of the action and require the user to confirm before completing the request.

5   Use defaults to minimize the number of user selections required to produce the most common or most likely outcome. For example, a chart program might require the user only to enter the numbers to be plotted on the chart. If nothing else is specified, the program plots the chart using judiciously chosen defaults for chart type (line, bar, pie chart), legends, labels, axes, and shading patterns.

Introduction to Guidelines
This first chapter was intended to summarize some general principles and strategies on which much of the specific guidance that follows in this book is based: The remainder of the book is organized and formatted as individual guidelines. Each guideline is numbered with a chapter number and an item number for ease of reference (2.1 for item 1 in chapter 2). Each also includes a short underlined caption to make the item easier to locate when the book is used as a handbook. Next, a short sentence in upper case summarizes the guideline succinctly. This "one-liner" is useful for preparing a checklist, locating a given guideline in the book, or just jogging one's memory after having read the book.

Next is the complete statement of the guideline with (hopefully) enough explanation to make it clear. If there are exceptions, tradeoffs, or other qualifying comments, they are included following the guideline statement. For many guidelines, examples of observing the guideline (labelled USE) and of failing to observe the guideline (labelled DON'T USE) are provided to make the suggestion more concrete.

General Human - Computer
Interface Concepts

Finally, references are given to authors who have provided recommendations, experimental results, or other information relevant to the guideline. Please note that the reference to a given author does not necessarily imply that the author would agree with the guideline as it has been interpreted and worded here. The reference is provided primarily to indicate that the guideline was influenced by this author's work and to provide a source for those who wish to investigate a particular guideline further.

Chapter Two
Designing Display Formats

In most human-computer interfaces the means of communicating information to the user is through a visual display device. The device itself, however, is only a medium — a blank slate. The design of the formats to be written on that slate is a critical determinant of the effectiveness with which the computer provides information to its users. The placement, organization, sequence, spacing, typography, and labelling used in display formats can all have a significant influence on the ease with which the users can notice, interpret, remember, and use the data presented. *Hendricks, Kilduff, Brooks, Marshak, and Doyle, 1982; Tullis, 1983*

Reserved Display Areas

Consistent use of fixed display locations or screen areas for the same information or the same kind of information is important in reducing search time and in aiding interpretation. Two kinds of fixed fields can be defined: invariant fields and functional category fields. *Teitelbaum and Granda, 1983*

2.1 Invariant Fields
Use invariant fields on each screen.

These are fields that stay the same on every page or screen. Fields such as the screen title, the screen identification, the page number, and the date are examples of invariant fields. Place such data on the same row and column range on every page. See Figure 2.1 for an example of a standardized format. *Engel and Granda, 1975 ; Galitz, 1981, 1985*

The standard header has ID, title, page number, and date -- all in standard locations on all formats.

```
ID = TER              Travel Expense Record              Page 1 of 1
                                                         July 15, 1986
TRAVEL ITINERARY

        Traveler's last name: _ _ _ _ _ _ _ _ _ _ _ _ _ _ _ _ _ _ _
           Traveler's initials: _ . _ .
    Departure date (MMDDYY): _ _ _ _ _ _
       Return date (MMDDYY): _ _ _ _ _ _
             Destination city: _ _ _ _ _ _ _ _ _ _ _ _ _ _ _ _ _ _ _
            Destination state: _ _

TRAVEL EXPENSES

    Meals: _ _ _ _ . _ _      Auto Rental: _ _ _ _ . _ _
    Lodging: _ _ _ _ . _ _      Air Fare: _ _ _ _ . _ _

Press ENTER to complete this form.

                                Next I D: _ _ _
```

The "Next ID" prompt appears on all formats in the same location.

Figure 2.1
Example of a Standardized Format

2.2 Functional Category Fields
Assign functional category fields.

These are fields reserved for particular kinds of data. A given kind of data may or may not be present on a given screen, but when it is present, the assigned screen location is used to display it. Examples of functional category fields include program messages, error messages, system messages, and alarms. (See Figure 2.1.) *Engel and Granda, 1975*

Consistent Conventions
Consistency is critical to effective display formatting. By following consistent conventions for procedures, terminology, formatting, and

Designing Display Formats

coding, we can provide the user with a familiar, predictable interface. The best way to ensure consistency is to establish and document a set of detailed design conventions early in a project. These local conventions may be based on general guidelines, such as those in this book, but they can be and should be more specific. Tailor the conventions to the capabilities, constraints, environment, and users of your system. Then enforce and maintain the conventions through management.

2.3 Procedures
Use standardized procedures.

To ensure consistency when the user must perform similar activities on different screens, certain procedural conventions are standardized. Sign-on and sign-off procedures, menu selection procedures, input procedures, and error correction procedures are examples of functions which require standardized conventions. *Engel and Granda, 1975; Galitz, 1981, 1985*

2.4 Use of Terms
Define and use terms consistently.

Once a term is defined, especially when it may have a common English meaning which is not intended, use the term consistently in the defined sense.

Example:
The word "screen" is generally understood by computer users to mean the contents of a display frame with a specific design and layout of information. The same word should not be used for the physical surface of the display. Other terms such as "display face" or "CRT faceplate" would be more appropriate and would eliminate potential ambiguity or confusion. *Brown et al., 1980, 1983*

2.5 Date Format
Follow the user's convention for the date format.

Use a date format that is consistent with the prevailing convention of the users. Julian date (year plus day of the year) is not familiar to most people (although it may be the standard date form for all the users of a given computer system). In most systems, dates should not be expressed in Julian format. *Peterson, 1979*

Local conventions also vary for the Gregorian date (day, month, year) in the order in which the components are shown and in the use of a month name (or abbreviation) versus a month number. For example, January tenth, 1985 may be represented as: 85-010, 01-10-85, Jan. 10,1985 , 10 Jan. 85, or 10-1-85. European conventions typically place the day before the month number, while Americans usually follow a month, day, year sequence. Where there is no consistent user convention, the use of a month name or month abbreviation eliminates potential ambiguity about which number is the month and which is the day.

2.6 User Conventions
Follow user's conventions for common data formats.

Use formats for common data, such as money and time of day that correspond to the conventions of the user community.

Example:
Computers often show time of day in a 24-hour clock format as a default, but many user groups are more familiar with a 12-hour clock format with A.M. or P.M. designated. For these users the time should be displayed in 12 hour format ("3:15 P.M.") rather than 24-hour format ("15:15").

2.7 Unique Format Identifiers
Each format has a unique ID.

In a computer system in which each transaction has a unique screen format, assign a unique ID to each screen or display format. A screen may have continuation pages that continue the same information beyond the space available on the original screen, usually in extended columnar form. Continuation pages all carry the ID of the "page 1" screen, and together they constitute a single entity as far as the user is concerned.

The unique screen format ID provides a convenient means for the user to:

1 identify which screen is being displayed,

2 request a specific screen without having to refer to a menu list, or

3 report trouble or identify the relevant screen in discussions.
   Brown et al., 1980, 1983; Patrick, 1980

Designing Display Formats

2.8 Format ID Design
Assign and use format IDs methodically.

Choose format identifiers that are short enough and meaningful enough to be learned and remembered easily. Display this alphanumeric code or mnemonic identifier in a standard location on all screens and continuation pages. It provides the basic means for moving in the system's screen hierarchy. See Figure 2.1 for an example. *Brown et al., 1980, 1983*

■ **Alphabetic Data**

The following guidelines can speed interpretation and reduce user errors in reading alphabetic data.

2.9 Left-justify Alphabetic Data
Left- justify lists of alphabetic data.

USE

| FORTRAN |
| APL |
| COBOL |
| PL1 |

DON'T USE

| FORTRAN |
| APL |
| COBOL |
| PL1 |

Engel and Granda, 1975 ; Galitz, 1981, 1985

2.10 Data Organization
Display lists of data in columns.

Organize long series of strings or lists of data in columns to provide better legibility and faster scanning.

USE

```
Job functions are:
- purchasing and procurement
- engineering systems and design
- general management
- manufacturing and quality control
```

DON'T USE

```
Job functions are purchasing and procurement,
engineering systems and design, general
management and manufacturing and quality control
```

2.11 Punctuation Conventions
Use conventional punctuation.

Use conventional English punctuation whenever possible. Don't arbitrarily use a punctuation mark or scheme that is counter to accepted English usage. When characters are required for delimiters or indicators in a computer dialogue, choose those most compatible with conventional punctuation. The appendix of Webster's New Collegiate Dictionary provides a convenient reference for English punctuation conventions. *Brown et al., 1983*

USE

```
Date must be 6 digits;
use MMDDYY format.
```

DON'T USE

```
Date must be 6 digits/
use MMDDYY format.
```

2.12 Prose Text
Use both upper and lower case for text .

Whenever the display equipment is capable of generating both cases, present text in upper and lower cases rather than all upper case. (Often the distinction between text and a label or a statement is that text has three or more lines of connected prose.) *Engel and Granda, 1975; Galitz, 1981, 1985; Hinsley and Hanes, 1977; Marcus, 1980, 1984; Seibel, 1972*

USE

> Longer text passages are easier to read when presented using standard capitalization rules rather than using all capital letters.

DON'T USE

> READING IN ALL CAPITAL LETTERS CAN TAKE LONGER BECAUSE WORDS LOSE THEIR CHARACTERISTIC SHAPES. ALL WORDS BECOME RECTANGULAR.

Exceptions:
When character visibility is marginal due to small character size or degraded viewing conditions, upper case text may be desirable to increase the effective character size. All upper case may also be useful in short captions, labels, or column headings to make the label distinct from the data.

2.13 Essential Information
Display only necessary information.

Display only the information that is necessary for the needs of the users' tasks. Avoid cluttering the screen with data that are irrelevant to the user. *Galitz, 1981, 1985*

USE

Please choose the data to be displayed.

CODE	DATA TYPE
1	Summary
2	Detailed list
3	Sequences

DON'T USE

Please choose the data to be displayed.

CODE	DATA TYPE	DATE IMPLEMENTED
1	Summary	5/16/79
2	Detailed list	6/18/79
3	Sequences	11/28/83

(Assuming that implementation date is irrelevant to users.)

Numeric Data
This section presents guidelines to speed interpretation and reduce user errors in reading and manipulating numeric data.

2.14 Punctuation
Punctuate long numeric fields.

Displays of long numeric fields are punctuated with spaces, commas, hyphens, slashes, or whatever is most appropriate. Use conventional punctuation schemes if they exist. If none exist, use a space between every third or fourth number. *Engel and Granda, 1975; Galitz, 1981, 1985; Seibel, 1972; Williges and Williges, 1981*

Example:

arbitrary numbers: phone numbers:

967 157 402   (407) 608-9732
842 772 953   (601) 878-4569
786 497 634   (808) 498-5421

social security numbers: numerical values or counts:

634-63-3223   5,879,642
625-83-2834   213,836,900
976-34-7654   67,735,034

dollar amounts:

$45,856.98
$865,945.86
$2,634,845.00

2.15   Right-Justify
Right-justify lists of numbers.

Right-justify lists of numbers without decimals. *Engel and Granda, 1975; Galitz, 1981, 1985*

USE   DON'T USE

124
34589
529
48

124
34589
529
48

2.16 Decimal Numbers
Lists containing decimals use decimal alignment.

Columns of numbers containing decimals are aligned on the decimal point.

Note:
Do not add or remove zeros arbitrarily after a decimal because, in some applications, the zeros may affect the meaning in terms of significant digits. *Brown et al., 1980, 1983*

USE   DON'T USE

| 1.5 |
| 15.98 |
| 645.760 |

| 1.5 |
| 15.98 |
| 645.760 |

Alphanumeric Codes
The term "code" is used here to refer to techniques that assign an alphanumeric symbol to stand for an item or function. Codes are typically used to provide a compact way to display or enter an item or function.

2.17 Code Structure
Letters and digits are properly grouped.

When designing an arbitrary code composed of both letters and digits, group the letters together and the digits together. When letters and digits are interspersed, errors in reading, remembering, and typing are more likely. The recommended structure is, for example, letter-letter-digit (HW5), not letter-digit-letter (H5W).

USE   DON'T USE

| FILE NUMBER |
| 159 BCE |
| 453 TPR |
| 938 PSD |

| FILE NUMBER |
| 1B5C9E |
| 4T5P3R |
| 9P3S8D |

Galitz, 1981, 1985

Designing Display Formats

2.18 One Case
Alphabetic codes use one case.

Use all upper-case or all lower-case letters within an arbitrary code that is made up of more than one letter. *Brown et al., 1980, 1983*

USE

```
ABCD
abcd
```

DON'T USE

```
AbCd
abCD
```

2.19 Selection Mnemonics
Use familiar mnemonic selection codes.

For selections with few options, single letter mnemonic codes such as the initial letter of the option name are easier to remember and use than item numbers.

USE

```
Enter sex
(F=female, M=male): __
```

DON'T USE

```
Enter Sex:___
1 Female
2 Male
```

Shinar, Stern, Bubis, and Ingram, 1985; Shneiderman, 1983a

2.20 Code Length
Use short codes.

Meaningless arbitrary codes that the user must remember or enter must be no longer than four alphabetic characters or five digits. The user will have trouble remembering the code and entering it correctly if it is any longer. Meaningful codes, such as one-word codes, can be longer without taxing memory because the word forms a single unit.

Example:
(When "Display ID" is entered by the user to request the next display.)

BEST

Display ID	Title
ARS	Accounts Receivable Summary
APS	Accounts Payable Summary
WPS	Weekly Payroll Summary

FAIR

Display ID	Title
147	Accounts Receivable Summary
365	Accounts Payable Summary
758	Weekly Payroll Summary

DON'T USE

Display ID	Title
NP002147	Accounts Receivable Summary
C6490365	Accounts Payable Summary
RS331758	Weekly Payroll Summary

Galitz, 1981, 1985

Layout of Data

The following paragraphs present conventions and principles of screen data formatting and systematic techniques for applying these principles. Layout characteristics of legibility, organization, clarity, and consistency of use and location are major design goals.

2.21 Data Order
Present lists of data in useful order.

Arrange the items in a list or on a menu in some recognizable and useful order (chronological, alphabetical, sequential, functional, by physical proximity, by frequency of use, or by importance). *Engel and Granda, 1975; Hinsley and Hanes, 1977*

Designing Display Formats

2.22 Data Grouping Strategies
Arrange data in logical groups.

Choose the most appropriate data grouping strategy, such as:

1 Sequential grouping. Sequential grouping is the arrangement of items in the temporal or spatial order in which they are usually used or encountered, such as on a printed form.

2 Functional grouping. Functional grouping is the arrangement of information according to its intended purpose or use. Categories of data that will be used together should be adjacent on the screen.

3 Importance grouping. Importance grouping is the arrangement of the most significant information, or that requiring immediate response, at the beginning or top of an array of data or list of selection choices.

4 Frequency grouping. Frequency grouping is the arrangement that places the most frequently used data or options at the beginning of a list of options or a table of data. This makes the commonly used data accessible more quickly. The user can find a frequently used option without searching through a series of rarely needed options.

2.23 Analogous Data
Present similar data in similar formats.

Use consistent screen layouts for presenting similar data on different screens. For example, do not present similar data in narrowly spaced vertical columns on one screen display and in widely spaced columns or in a horizontal list on another display.

2.24 Location
Use consistent data locations.

Present a given type of information in the same location from screen to screen. The user can read and interpret data faster if they are presented in a predictable, familiar arrangement. *Engel and Granda, 1975; Galitz 1981, 1985; MIL-STD-1472C, 1981*

Example:
If there is a line of system status data that appears on several displays, place it in the same location on all these displays.

2.25 Data Differentiation
Make instructions distinct from data.

Arrange data on display screens in such a way as to differentiate between instructions and data. Use consistent locations for each to help distinguish instructions from data.

2.26 Instructions Location
Locate instructions in sequence.

Place instructions according to the order in which they are performed. Locate instructions to start a transaction near the top of the screen or window. Place instructions to complete a transaction near the bottom. Place instructions that refer to a specific entry prompt immediately preceding that prompt. *Galitz, 1981, 1985*

33

2.27 Data Relationships
Arrange data to make relationships clear.

Display data on the screen to facilitate observation of task-relevant similarities, differences, trends, and relationships among the data. Several techniques that may be useful for showing data relationships are:

1   arrangement for proximity among related elements,

2   use of boxes or lines to group elements, or

3   use of color or highlighting techniques to unite related elements.

Example:

Costs ($)			Production	(Units)	
Actual	Predicted	Difference	Actual	Predicted	Difference
967	907	+60	83	82	+1
721	777	-56	57	54	+3
475	471	+4	91	95	-4

2.28 Labeling
Label each data field.

Label every data field with a caption or column heading to identify the item and to reduce memorization requirements.

Exception:
When all users can be expected to be experts and frequent users, less labeling may be acceptable. The space saved on labeling may allow more data to be displayed. This can be of more value than labels to experts in some situations, such as air traffic control, stock market ticker-tape, and so on. *Engel and Granda, 1975; Galitz, 1981, 1985*

USE

QSR	QUARTERLY SALES REPORT		Page 1 of 1
MONTH	UNITS SOLD	COSTS X $1000	PROFITS X $1000
1	246	23	13
2	221	18	17
3	266	20	25
NEXT ID: _ _ _			

DON'T USE

QSR	QUARTERLY SALES REPORT		Page 1 of 1
1	246	23	13
2	221	18	17
3	266	20	25
NEXT ID: _ _ _			

2.29 Consistent Labels
Position labels consistently.

Establish and maintain a constant relationship between labels and their associated data fields. In tables of data with column heading labels, left-justifying the header over the column of data can provide an effective cue to the location of the boundary of the column. However, sometimes a numeric data field must be designed to accommodate many more digits (for the largest number anticipated) than are typically used. Left-justifying the label over a column of this kind of data can cause the column of numbers, with leading zeros suppressed, to appear dissociated from its heading. Right-justification of the header may be more appropriate in this case. *Brown, 1981, 1982; Brown et al, 1980,1983; Frey, Sides, Hunt, and Rouse, 1983*

see example on page 38

Designing Display Formats

USE

NAME	DEPARTMENT	PHONE	$DUE
Barnes, H.J.	C-768	634-2389	78.39
Jones, K.T.	W-304	634-5632	149.33
Parnell, N.B.	D-243	634-9247	203.87
Tyler, S.D.	D-254	634-9509	1367.90

DON'T USE

NAME	DEPARTMENT	PHONE	$DUE
Barnes, H.J.	C-768	634-2389	78.39
Jones, K.T.	W-304	634-5632	149.33
Parnell, N.B.	D-243	634-9247	203.87
Tyler, S.D.	D-254	634-9509	1367.90

2.30 Units
Show unit used for each variable.

Display the units for data fields or column headings. For example:

USE

Time (s)	Velocity (ft/s)	Temperature (degrees C)
5	9	24
21	49	29

DON'T USE

Time	Velocity	Temperature
5	9	24
21	21	29

Patrick, 1980

2.31 Paper Form Entry
Make screens correspond to report forms.

If data are to be entered from paper forms, design the layout of the input screen and the paper form to correspond. This helps the user to find and keep a location while looking back and forth from the paper form to the terminal.

Designing the paper form to correspond to the screen format requirements is often desirable because screen formatting is typically more constrained by space limitations than is paper form design. If redesign of the paper form is not feasible, design the entry screen format to correspond to the paper form. *Galitz, 1981, 1985; Patrick,1980; Peterson, 1979; Seibel, 1972*

2.32 Clutter
Keep displays uncluttered.

Avoid overcrowded and cluttered displays. Clutter is caused by lack of order, by poor spacing, and by displaying unnecessary data. Present data using spacing or grouping or in columns to produce an orderly and legible display. Do not try to present too much data on a single screen. Distribute the unused area to separate logical groups rather than having all unused area on one side.

Tullis (1983) reviewed the literature on display formatting and suggested the following:

1 There is an optimal density for a given display, and densities either higher or lower than the optimum may degrade user performance.

2 Displays using 15 percent of the available character positions may be optimal.

3 Increasing the display density from 15 to 25 percent may have a minimal adverse effect on user performance, but densities over 25 percent may degrade performance.

Designing Display Formats

Exception:

In systems that are designed for use by highly skilled frequent users who require quick access to large quantities of data, denser displays may be preferable. For example, air traffic controllers need access to a complete display of nearby traffic at all times, even if this requires extremely dense displays.

2.33 Spacing to Group
Use blank lines to separate groups of lines.

Use blank lines to separate and partition related groups of data. A blank row inserted after every four or five lines in a table of data can also enhance the readability of the table. Visually scanning a row of data across its columns is easier because the blank line reduces the chances that a user will start scanning on one row and inadvertently read later columns from a different row.

USE

DEPT.	MANAGER	BUILDING	REGION
D4989	Patel, R.J.	701-S	Northeast
F9032	Thomas, B.G.	599	North Central
D3487	Bronson, G.S.	499-N	Southwest
E5391	Whiting, R.P.	323	Central
R5885	Jackson, D.D.	657	Southwest
F4352	Smith, C.P.	987	Central
R7099	Victor, K.T.	295-W	East
T5629	Gladstone, A.T.	921	North
J6873	Jenson, S.D.	340-S	Central

DON'T USE

DEPT.	MANAGER	BUILDING	REGION
D4989	Patel, R.J.	701-S	Northeast
F9032	Thomas, B.G.	599	North Central
D3487	Bronson, G.S.	499-N	Southwest
E5391	Whiting, R.P.	323	Central
R5885	Jackson, D.D.	657	Southwest
F4352	Smith, C.P.	987	Central
R7099	Victor, K.T.	295-W	East
T5629	Gladstone, A.T.	921	North
J6873	Jenson, S.D.	340-S	Central

Designing Display Formats

Tradeoffs:

When an application requires that as many rows as possible be displayed on the same screen, the designer must weigh the increased readability gained by spacing against the loss of a few lines of data. Placing the columns closer together can also make reading across a row easier. *Galitz, 1981*

2.34 Display Selection Field
Locate selection fields consistently.

When display selection is accomplished by typing an alphanumeric code into a selection entry field,make the location of the selection field consistent for all displays. *Brown, 1981, 1982; Brown et al., 1980, 1983*

Example:

The "NEXT ID: _ _ _" field from the USE/DON'T USE examples in previous guidelines should be in the same location on all screens or windows that use it.

2.35 Protected Areas
Make non-entry fields protected.

Areas of the display not needed for data entry are inaccessible to the user. Labels, headings, prompts, instructions, and blank areas are skipped by automatic cursor control.

Lists

A list is a common and useful way to present related items and options to users. The guidelines to follow offer some ways to make lists clear and usable. Since menus are special cases of lists, some of these items apply to menus. Guidelines that relate more exclusively to menus are included in the menu section of Chapter 6, Dialogue Design.

2.36 List Heading

A list heading defines the list.

Each list of selection should have a heading, caption, or prompt that reflects the question for which an answer is sought.

USE   DON'T USE

41

```
ORGANIZATION TYPE          |   R = Responsible
                           |   P = Performing
R = Responsible            |   A = Assigned
P = Performing             |
A = Assigned               |
```

Engel and Granda, 1975

2.37 List Form

List items one to a line.

When listing or enumerating items, each one should start on a new line.

USE   DON'T USE

```
Available options are      |   Available options are1.Choose
1. Choose new subset       |   new subset,  2. Select data,
2. Select data             |   3. Write to file
3. Write to file           |
```

Engel and Granda, 1975

Exception:
To identify the codes for two to four options stated in one or two words each, it may be preferable to attach the code definitions to the field label. This may be a more effective use of limited screen space in some situations.

Example:

PERSONNEL CATEGORY (H=HOURLY, S=SALARIED)

2.38 Item Enumeration
Enumerate items with numbers, not letters.

If arbitrary item identifiers are used to enumerate a list, integer numbers starting with 1 for the first item are preferable to sequential alphabetic enumeration.

USE

DON'T USE

Select next action
1. Choose new subset
2. Select data
3. Write to file

Available options:
A. Choose new subset
B. Select data
C. Write to file

Engel and Granda, 1975

Note:
For short menu selection lists, mnemonic alphabetic codes may often be preferable to sequential letters or numbers. *Perlman, 1984; Shneiderman, 1983a, 1986*

Example:

Select next action: _
N = New subset
D = Data selection
W = Write to file

2.39 Option Listing
List common options first.

In a list of options, place the most frequently used options at the beginning of the list. *Engel and Granda, 1975*

USE   DON'T USE

VEHICLE TYPE
1. Passenger car
2. Pick-up truck
3. Bus

VEHICLE TYPE
1. Passenger car
2. Bus
3. Pick-up truck

2.40 Text Descriptors
Separate item numbers from text.

Separate selection numbers from text descriptors by at least one space. Include the space after the period, if used. Right-justify selection numbers.

USE   DON'T USE

Available options
1. Choose new subset.
2. Select data
3. Write file.

Available options
1Choose new subset.
2Select data
3 Write file.

Engel and Granda, 1975

2.41 Headings for Multiple Pages
Display headings on each page.

When a tabular display must be paged for continuation, column headings and row labels are displayed on every page, not just the first page. This reduces the chance of user confusion and provides a complete record if a hardcopy is printed.

2.42   Variable-Length Listing
Provide continuation page indicators.

Lists or data tables often extend beyond what can be shown on one display page. The user must be informed when a list is or is not complete. Unless the list is short and it is obvious that it does not fill the available space, it is marked with the message --END OF LIST--. Incomplete lists are marked --CONTINUED ON NEXT PAGE--. If the message is too long and it would reduce the display capacity, it may be shortened to --CONTINUED--. *Patrick, 1980*

USE

(First Page)   (Next Page)

```
NAME                          NAME
J. J. Jackson                 S.S. Stevens
M. T. Barnes                  P.R. Townes
F. D. Smith
J. P. BlACK
--CONTINUED--                 -END OF LIST-
```

A page indicator, such as PAGE 1 OF 2 or PAGE 1 (MORE) may also be used to indicate continuation. For example:

OR USE

(First page)   (Next page)

```
NAME            Page 1 of 2    NAME            Page 2 of 2

J. J. Jackson                  S.S. Stevens
M. T. Barnes                   P.R. Townes
F. D. Smith
J. P. Black
```

OR USE

(First page)

```
NAME          Page 1        (More)

J. J. Jackson
M. T. Barnes
F. D. Smith
J. P. BlACK
```

(Next page)

```
NAME          Page 2        (Last)

S.S. Stevens
P.R. Townes
```

DON'T USE

(First page)

```
NAME          Page 1        (More)

J. J. Jackson
M. T. Barnes
F. D. Smith
J. P. BlACK
```

(Next page)

```
NAME          Page 2        (Last)

S.S. Stevens
P.R. Townes
```

Highlighting

Highlighting techniques can be useful in drawing attention to specific areas of a display if these techniques are properly applied. Highlighting refers to a variety of display techniques used to make selected items stand out from other displayed items. The effectiveness of highlighting in drawing attention to important or unusual data depends on the extent to which highlighted data are exceptions to the perceptual norm. This implies that if too many items are highlighted in the same display, none of them will stand out. In the extreme, if "highlighting" becomes the norm, the unhighlighted items may actually stand out more than the highlighted ones.

Common examples of highlighting include the following diversions from the typical display style:

1 increased brightness,

2 color,

3 reverse video,

4 atypical fonts, type size, italics, or boldface,

5 underscores or boxes around target items,

6 all capital letters in typically mixed case text, or

7 blinking of target items. *Engel and Granda, 1975*

2.43 Uses of Highlighting
Use highlighting to draw attention.

Highlighting is useful to call attention to critical screen components, such as items being operated upon, fields containing errors, error messages, critical items, or critical instructions.

2.44 Highlight Sparingly
Use highlighting sparingly.

Highlight only a small proportion of the data on a given screen. Highlighting is most effective for adding emphasis to a set of data when the screen is relatively uniform except for a small amount of highlighted data. When highlighting is accomplished either by increasing the brightness or by displaying highlighted data in the color white, overuse can lead to unacceptable overall display brightness and to visual discomfort. *Galitz, 1981*

2.45 Selection Highlighting
Highlight selected items.

Use highlighting to indicate which item in a list has been selected. This is especially important in certain situations:

1 where combinations of choices can be made ("Pick 2 from column A, 3 from column B, and 1 from column C."), feedback is needed to show the overall pattern of choices, or

2 where pointing devices are used for selection (light pen, mouse, or touch panel), feedback is needed to verify that the intended option was actually selected.

Example:
A menu of options is presented for selection on a touch panel device. When the user touches an item, its label inverts from normal video (light characters on a dark background) to reverse video (dark characters on a light background). *Engel and Granda, 1975*

2.46 Blink Coding
Use blink coding sparingly.

Blink coding (flashing) is used sparingly for well-defined special meanings, such as alarms. Although blinking is quite effective at drawing attention, many users find blinking to be distracting and annoying. Allow the blinking to be cancelled by the operator as an acknowledgement of the signal. Data that must be read and interpreted by the user must not blink because blinking makes data hard to read. Use blinking in an adjacent field, such as a blinking symbol prefix or a blinking box around the data, to draw attention to the message. *Engel and Granda, 1975; Galitz, 1981; Smith and Goodwin, 1972*

47

Exception:
A blinking insertion point cursor symbol may be very useful in helping the user to locate the current pointer location, especially in word processing or other applications in which the cursor might otherwise be difficult to locate. *Savage, Habinek, and Blackstad, 1982; Smith and Mosier, 1984*

2.47 Blink Levels
Use only two levels of blink coding.

Do not use differing blink rates to represent different categories of data. Use only two levels (blinking and not blinking) of blink coding. Differences in blink rates are not reliably discriminable. *Smith and Mosier, 1984*

Note:
Engel and Granda (1975) suggest that three levels of blinking (none, slow, and fast) are acceptable, but I recommend this only in unusual circumstances. If slow and fast blinking are considered necessary, do not make critical decisions contingent upon discriminating whether an item is blinking slowly or quickly.

2.48 Blink Rate
Use a 2 to 5 Hertz blink rate.

The recommended blink rate is 2 to 5 times per second, with a nominal duty cycle (time"on") of 50 percent.

2.49 Brightness Highlighting
Use only two levels of brightness coding.

Use only two brightness levels for coding: normal brightness and enhanced brightness. To use more levels would risk degrading the visibility of low brightness categories or creating categories that may not be reliably discriminable. *Engel and Granda, 1975; Smith and Mosier, 1984*

2.50 Reverse Video Highlighting
Check legibility of reverse video.

Some display devices may be less legible in reverse video unless the font design is appropriate for dark-on-light. Two kinds of problems can occur, but both can usually be eliminated.

1   The bright area around a character may "bloom" inward on some monitors, reducing the effective stroke width of the character. If reduced legibility results, it can be corrected by using a bolder character font for reverse video characters. (Of course, some display devices do not support multiple fonts.)

2   With color monitors a black character on a colored background (the standard reverse video technique) might suffer reduced legibility in some colors on some monitors. A white character on a colored background may be a better choice for reverse video with certain colors (red is a common example).

3   The occurrence and nature of legibility and color contrast problems varies considerably with different display monitors. The best advice is to check the planned reverse video approach for legibility on the monitors to be used. If poor legibility results, change the font or color of the characters.

Example:
In a process control application, the labels of monitored events are displayed in either green, yellow, or red to indicate the criticality of the event. When an event occurs, its label changes from normal (green, yellow, or red characters on a black background) to reverse video (the background becomes green, yellow, or red). White and black are both neutral colors with no assigned meaning in the system's color code. Because a red background produces poor visibility with black characters, the designers use white on red reverse video when a "red" event occurs.

49

Chapter Three
Effective Wording

The choice of wording and codes and the manner of presenting them should follow principles of legibility, brevity, clarity, and consistency. Careful selection of wording can produce many advantages. Ambiguity and confusion are minimized, and performance is faster and more accurate. The principles of standardization and consistency of language and coding apply not only within a displayed screen, but also within a module, an application program, and an entire information processing system. For a large corporation's information processing system, conventions for wording, coding, definitions, and procedures should be standardized at the company level. When users are forced to adapt to different conventions for each of several application programs, accuracy and efficiency suffer.

Abbreviations

Abbreviations are used both for display of data to the user and for entry of data and commands by the user. Most of the following guidelines apply to the abbreviation of computer output display data. A different set of concerns apply to abbreviation of data entered by the user. Chapter Seven (Data Entry) presents more abbreviation guidelines for input. Chapter Six (Dialogue Design) presents abbreviation guidelines for commands.

In human-computer interface design, abbreviation of displayed data is often necessary to permit the required data and their labels to fit on a limited amount of screen space. Each abbreviation should be short, meaningful, and distinct from other abbreviations used. Resist the temptation to use abbreviations the user is not likely to understand or remember just to make room for more data on the display.

3.1 Length of Abbreviations
Use abbreviations only if they are significantly shorter.

Do not abbreviate unless either the abbreviation is significantly shorter than the full word or it is more meaningful to the user than the full word. If the abbreviation will only save one or two characters, use the unabbreviated word. *Engel and Granda, 1975; Galitz, 1981*

3.2 Consistent Abbreviations
Use only one abbreviation for a word.

Do not arbitrarily abbreviate the same word differently in different places, pages, or levels of the system.

Exception:
Exceptions may be necessary for the column headings of data in tables when the columns cannot be separated enough to permit the standard abbreviation of the heading.

3.3 Abbreviation Rules
Use consistent abbreviation rules.

Follow a rule or set of rules for selecting command abbreviations. Truncation rules have been recommended by Ehrenreich (1981). Truncation is the deletion of letters from the end of the word. Grudin and Barnard (1984, 1985) suggest, however, that the best abbreviation strategy may depend on whether the user is trying to construct the correct abbreviation from the word (encoding) or trying to recognize a word from its abbreviation (decoding) . Encoding is required to use abbreviations as type-in commands. Decoding is required to interpret abbreviated labels, captions, or data on a display.

In a subsequent survey of abbreviation experiments, Ehrenreich (1985) concluded that encoding an abbreviation is easier when a simple abbreviation rule is followed and taught to the user. Truncation has consistently proven to be the abbreviation rule of choice for encoding (remembering the abbreviation given the word). Decoding (remembering what a given abbreviation stands for), however, has not shown the same advantage for truncation rules.

3.4 Dictionary of Abbreviations
Provide a dictionary of definitions.

Compile a dictionary of abbreviations for user reference in online and printed documentation.

3.5 Unnecessary Abbreviations
Abbreviate only when necessary.

Do not abbreviate computer-generated data unless

1 it is necessary for proper alignment,

2 there is not enough room to spell out the word, or

3 the users understand the abbreviation better than the spelled out word.

For example, "FORTRAN" may be more recognizable than "Formula Translation Language". *Engel and Granda, 1975; Galitz, 1981; Hinsley and Hanes, 1977*

Note:
This guideline applies to the abbreviation of words that are output by a computer for display to users. In many applications the ability to abbreviate inputs to a computer system is desirable to reduce the number of key strokes required of users .

3.6 Common Abbreviations
Avoid obscure abbreviations.

If space must be conserved, abbreviate commonly abbreviated terms rather than words that will result in obscure abbreviations. For example, to abbreviate RESTRICTED PROCESS ACCOUNT NUMBER (when limited space forces abbreviation):

USE

RESTRICTED PROCESS ACCT NO

DON'T USE

RESTR PROC ACCOUNT NUMBER

3.7 Multiple Abbreviations
Avoid multiple abbreviations.

Abbreviating several words in a single phrase, prompt, heading, or command can compound the potential for ambiguity and misinterpretation. When limited space forces multiple abbreviations in the same phrase, consider potential misinterpretations and choose abbreviations to minimize them.

3.8 Abbreviation Definition
Define abbreviations on the same screen.

When a term is spelled out at one place on a screen and abbreviated in other places, show the abbreviation in parentheses after the spelled-out version if enough space is available. For example:

```
┌─────────────────────────────────────────────┐
│          LINE OF BUSINESS (LOB)             │
│                                             │
│      CONTRACT:_ _ _ _ _ _ _    LOB:_ _ _ _ _ _ │
│                                             │
└─────────────────────────────────────────────┘
```

3.9 Hyphenation
Lines end with whole words.

Minimize the hyphenation of words for continuation. The entire word should be placed on one line in electronic displays. *Engel and Granda, 1975; Galitz, 1981; Peterson, 1979*

USE

```
┌─────────────────────────┐
│ Do not hyphenate        │
│ for continuation.       │
│                         │
└─────────────────────────┘
```

DON'T USE

```
┌─────────────────────────┐
│ Do not hyphenate for con-│
│ tinuation               │
│                         │
└─────────────────────────┘
```

Exception:
This does not apply to word processing applications, which should display the text on the screen exactly as it will subsequently appear on the printed page.

3.10 Broken Sentences
Complete a sentence on the same screen.

When displaying text, instructions, or help in full-screen or full-window pages and scrolling is not possible, end each screen in a complete sentence. If a sentence begins on one screen or page and ends on the next, users may forget the first half of the sentence by the time they enter a page command and wait for the display to change pages.

Exceptions:
If scrolling functions are available or if the application is word processing, this may not apply.

3.11 Usable Information
Present information in the form that it is used.

Present information in directly usable form. Do not require the user to refer to documentation or to translate, transpose, change units, or interpolate.

USE	DON'T USE
The NAME must contain letters only, not numbers.	Edit Error 43M-T7Y. Refer to manual 4369B.

Engel and Granda, 1975

3.12 Standards and Conventions
Follow appropriate user conventions.

Use standards and conventions that are appropriate to the user. For example, time is expressed in a 12-hour clock with A.M. and P.M. designations for most civilian users. A 24-hour clock, 0001 to 2400, however, is used by the military. If users work with English units of measurement, do not present data in metric units or vice versa. Computer clock or date data that are not in useful form for the users are displayed only after conversion to a form familiar to users. For example, the Julian data conventions (yy-ddd) used by many computer systems is inappropriate for most users. Because of possible ambiguities in other forms, the DA MON YR form of date, 30 APR 85, is recommended.
Engel and Granda, 1975

3.13 Labels
Use clear labels to describe data.

When choosing headings or labels for fields or columns of data, use distinct and meaningful words that describe the data and distinguish the label from other labels.

USE

```
┌─────────────────────────────┐
│ A=ADD, C=CHANGE: _          │
└─────────────────────────────┘
```

DON'T USE

```
┌─────────────────────────────┐
│ FUNCTION CODE: _             │
└─────────────────────────────┘
```

Engel and Granda, 1975; Galitz, 1981

Coding
Coding is the creation of a special language for convenience or brevity. Like abbreviations, there are ways to make codes easier for users to learn, use, and remember.

3.14 Coding Consistency
Use consistent codes.

Like abbreviations, the meanings of symbols and codes remain unchanged from page to page. Use a coding scheme that provides a single unique code for each coded element.

3.15 Meaningful Codes
Use meaningful codes.

Use meaningful codes or words in preference to arbitrary codes. For example, a three-letter meaningful mnemonic code is easier to remember and use than a three-digit numeric code. *Elam, 1980*

USE

```
┌─────────────────────────────┐
│ DIR   Directory Listing     │
│ REW   Rewind File           │
└─────────────────────────────┘
```

DON'T USE

```
┌─────────────────────────────┐
│ 379 Directory Listing       │
│ 742 Rewind File             │
└─────────────────────────────┘
```

Terminology

Terms that are selected carefully and used in consistent ways will ease the users' tasks and simplify the training of operators.

3.16 Familiar Terminology

Use familiar terms.

Avoid difficult words, abbreviations, and acronyms that are not commonly used by all system users.

USE

DON'T USE

These data require a special access code. Please call Data Administration at extension 2985	IMS/VS DBMS CLASS IV DATA. SEE DBSA, W75B37-59

3.17 Term Definition

Define terms carefully.

The terms used on the displays are fully defined in the documentation. Terms that are technical, that can have more than one meaning, or that are used in a more specific sense than their usual English meaning should be defined explicitly, noting the connotation intended.

The choice of a word for a particular connotation must be based on the meaning that the word is likely to convey to a user, which may be different from a programmer's or a system designer's meaning. The programmer must adapt computer dialog to the user's vocabulary, not force the user to adapt to the programmer's vocabulary. There are other related considerations:

1 Do not use words the user is not likely to know.

2 Do not use a word that is likely to be interpreted differently than intended.

3 Do not use the same term to mean different things at different stages in the dialog.

4 Do not arbitrarily use different terms to mean the same thing at different stages in the dialog.

5　Do not use longer words than necessary; do not use inflated, formal language.

6　Do not assume operator training will cover terms and words that are obscure or used with special meanings in a computer-based system.

Engel and Granda, 1975

3.18 Technical Jargon
Minimize the use of jargon.

If a word is likely to be unfamiliar to the least skilled user, do not use it. When programmers or system designers format displays for less technical users, they typically find it difficult to think in the vocabulary of the user. This leads to wording that the user perceives as "computerese". Many users will be confused or intimidated by overly technical or esoteric terminology. The basic rule should be to know the users and adapt the screen dialog to their vocabulary instead of forcing them to learn a new vocabulary. *Engel and Granda, 1975*

3.19　Consistent Wording
Use consistent wording.

Use consistent and uniform wording and coding. For example, the title of a display should be identical in wording to the menu option used to call it ("choose data" in the example below). *Engel and Granda, 1975*

USE　(In a 2 menu sequence:)

(First menu)

```
NEXT ACTION
C.  Choose data
W.  Write file


Selection: C
```

(The user selects C for "Choose data".)

(Second menu)
(The requested menu appears with the same wording in the title as the selected option on the previous menu.)

```
CHOOSE DATA
N. Name
A. Address
P. Phone Number

Selection:
```

DON'T USE (In a 2 menu sequence:)
(First menu)

```
NEXT ACTION
 C. Choose data
W. Write file

Selection: C
```

(The user selects C for "Choose data".)

(Second menu)
(The requested menu appears but the wording in the title is different than the option name on the previous menu.)

```
DATA SELECTION
1. Name
2. Address
3. Phone Number

Selection: _
```

3.20 Interpretation
Use unambiguous words.

Avoid words or phrases that may be interpreted in more than one way. Some terms have a special meaning to data processing personnel, but users may interpret the terms in the more general (layman's) sense.

USE

> THE COMPUTER SYSTEM WILL BE DOWN FOR SERVICE UNTIL
> ABOUT 4:00 PM

DON'T USE

> SESSION NOT BOUND

Grammar and Sentence Structure

Simple grammatical structure and short sentences are interpreted more quickly and accurately. Long sentences with multiple clauses are likely to be confusing. In general, short, descriptive, active voice sentences are read faster and interpreted more easily. *Broadbent, 1977; Engel and Granda, 1975; Galitz, 1981*

3.21 Structure

Use short simple sentences.

Simple sentence structure is used, and long sentences are avoided by breaking them into two or more statements. Simple, descriptive words also are used wherever possible.*Chapanis, 1965; Engel and Granda, 1975; Galitz, 1981; Wright and Barnard, 1975*

3.22 Main Topic

Begin sentences with the main topic.

Place the main topic of a sentence near the beginning of the sentence.

USE

> To start the print sequence, enter the PRINT FILE command and specify
> the print options and the type of printer you have.

DON'T USE

> Enter the PRINT FILE command and specify the print options and the
> type of printer you have to start the print sequence.

3.23 Affirmative Statements
Use affirmative statements.

Statements made in the affirmative are more easily understood than negative statements. Tell what to do, rather than what to avoid.
Broadbent, 1977; Galitz, 1981; Wright and Barnard, 1975

USE

> Clear the screen before
> entering data.

DON'T USE

> Do not enter data before
> clearing the screen.

3.24 Consistent Construction
Use consistent statement structure.

Use consistent grammatical constructions for titles and headings. For example, do not use short sentences for some items and single words or phrases for others.

USE

> Select:
> 1. Choose data
> 2. Erase screen
> 3. Write file

DON'T USE

> Select:
> 1. Choose data
> 2. Screen erasure function
> 3. Write file

3.25 Active Sentences
State sentences in the active voice.

Readers usually understand active voice sentences more easily than passive voice sentences. *Chapanis, 1965; Broadbent, 1977*

USE

> Clear the screen by
>   pressing RESET.

DON'T USE

> The screen is cleared
> pressing RESET

3.26 Temporal Sequence
Describe steps in order of use.

If a sentence describes a sequence of instructions or events, the word order in the sentence should correspond to the temporal sequence of events. *Broadbent, 1977; Galitz, 1981; Wright and Barnard, 1975*

USE

> Enter LOGON sequence
> before running programs.

DON'T USE

> Before running programs,
> exit LOGON sequence

3.27 Conversational Language
Use a conversational language style.

Avoid the tendency to use overly formal styles of language and grammar. Use standard, grammatically correct, informal wording. "Conversational language" implies the following:

1   It is acceptable to address the user as "you" (second person). In fact, this is often the most natural and easily understood way to state instructions. However, refer to the computer system in the third person, not in the first person. Users may resent a dialogue which refers to the computer as if it were a person.

2   In conversations we speak predominately in the present tense and active voice.

3   In conversations we use "please", "thank you", and other standard courtesies. *Dean, 1982*

USE

Please enter your personal identification number.

DON'T USE

PERSONAL IDENTIFICATION NUMBER MUST NOW BE ENTERED.

DON'T USE

I NEED YOUR PERSONAL IDENTIFICATION NUMBER. ENTER IT NOW.

Chapter Four
Color

Many display terminals have a color capability. This color capability, when applied properly, may aid user-computer interactions by allowing users to locate or identify classes of displayed information with greater speed and reliability.

Color cathode ray tube (CRT) display terminals employ the three primary colors of light: red, blue, and green. They are used singly or in combination to produce color images. The primary colors may be presented alone to display data in red, blue, or green, or in combinations to produce other colors: red plus blue produces pink (or magenta), red and green produce yellow, blue and green produce turquoise (or cyan), and all three primaries together produce white.

Color is a highly salient feature of a stimulus in human visual perception. Variations in color are therefore highly effective in drawing attention. Whether this characteristic of color is a blessing or a curse to the user of a display system depends upon the skill of the designer in using colors in a task-related way. If colors are chosen to guide the user's attention to task-relevant aspects of the dialogue, color can have a significant beneficial effect on the user's productivity and satisfaction. On the other hand, if color is used in a capricious way, or even in a logical way that is not task-related, the user's attention may be drawn to irrelevant aspects of the dialog.

Appropriate Uses for Color
Color can be effectively used for many purposes if it is implemented carefully and conservatively. These uses include emphasizing or deemphasizing data, relating separated fields of data to each other, differentiating data, identifying or categorizing information, and assisting in searching for items or categories of data. *Galitz,1981*

The effective use of color requires consideration of several kinds of factors:

1 The impact of the selected color code on the legibility of the displayed data.

2 The cognitive effects of the color code on the performance of the user's tasks.

3 The impact of capabilities and limitations of the display medium. Consideration of the first two factors is reflected in the guidelines to follow in this chapter. Consideration of the third item can often lead to tailoring some of the guidelines for specific systems.

The display medium to be used often offers opportunities to the designer. For example, the enhanced capabilities and declining prices of modern color displays are making the conclusions of some earlier reports questioning the cost-effectiveness of color over monochrome seem dated. Also, many systems can generate hundreds of variations in the hue and saturation of colors. Thus, colors that traditionally exhibited legibility problems in older systems can be replaced with judiciously chosen colors from a much larger palette. For example, the saturated ("deep") blue, which often is hard to read on a CRT display, can be replaced with a desaturated ("light") blue to alleviate the legibility problems. Colors that are often confused with each other by color-weak users can be replaced by colors that are more discernible to those with weak color perception, yet are called by the same names as the original colors by color-normal users.

The characteristics of display media also present constraints to the designer. First, the design must accommodate the least-capable display device that any user may use. For example, if monochrome displays may be used by some users, the designer must ensure that no important information is conveyed by color alone. Second, the designer must recognize and design for device-specific color, brightness, and contrast effects. General rules of thumb may need modification to account for the eccentricities of a particular device. The best advice is to try a candidate color code on the target device(s) before finalizing it. Finally, the designer must not consider the capability of a device to display hundreds of colors as a mandate to use as many colors as possible in each format. Using color conservatively is one of the key approaches to using it effectively.

4.1 Overuse of Color
Use color conservatively.

Use color conservatively in the design of display formats. Arbitrary use of multiple colors may cause the screen to appear busy or cluttered, and may reduce the likelihood that the truly useful information in color codes on that format or on other formats will be interpreted appropriately and quickly. Because color changes are attention-getting, color variations that are not relevant to performance of the user's task are likely to be more

distracting than helpful. In general, additional colors should be added to the base color display only if they will help the user in performing a task. Overuse of color can produce displays that are more difficult to use than the monochromatic equivalents.
Frey, Sides, Hunt, and Rouse, 1983; Krebs, Wolf, and Sandvig, 1978

4.2 Color for Search
Use color for search tasks.

Locating a particular value or category of data on a display is faster if the target item is a different color than most of the rest of the display. The greater the display density, the more beneficial color coding can be .

The benefits of color for search tasks decrease:

1   as the number of nontarget items in the target's color increases,

2   if the user does not know the color of the target item in advance, and

3   if nontargets are shown in colors similar to the target's color.
   Carter, 1979 ; Christ, 1975; Krebs, Wolf, and Sandvig, 1978; Smith, 1962,1963; Teichner, Christ, and Corso, 1977

4.3 Color for Emphasis
Use color to highlight.

Variations in color attract considerable attention. For this reason, color is extremely effective for highlighting related data that are spread around on a display, such as data of a particular status or category. Color may effectively aid in the location of headings, out-of-tolerance data, newly entered data, and data requiring attention. *Durrett and Trezona, 1982; Galitz, 1981; Teichner, Christ, and Corso,1977*

4.4 Color for Status
Use color to indicate status.

Color can be effectively employed to show the status of displayed data. For example, a parameter value can be displayed in green when the parameter is within its normal, safe range, change to yellow when the parameter reaches marginally safe values, and change to red when it exceeds safe limits. *MIL-STD-1472C, 1981*

Chapter Four

4.5 Adding Color to Displays
Add color to a well-formatted display.

In designing a screen, apply color as an additional aid to the user. However, the format should be designed so that it is effective when displayed in a single color. Do not use color in an attempt to compensate for a poorly-formatted display.
Brown et al, 1980, 1983

4.6 Monochrome-Compatibility
Make color codes redundant with other codes.

Do not convey information solely by color if the information may be viewed from monochromatic as well as color terminals or when color may be lost in printed screen-image hardcopy. When both kinds of terminals may beused, limit color to assisting the user of the color terminal by highlighting, aiding in categorization, or clarifying the relationships of data, without sacrificing important information to the user of the monochromatic display or printout. Redundant coding techniques (such as using reverse video, underlining, boxing-in, fill patterns, or flashing) in conjunction with color, can provide the same information to monochrome terminals as to color terminals. *Brown et al., 1980, 1983; Krebs, Wolf, and Sandvig, 1978; Robertson, 1980*

4.7 Color Registration
Consider color registration.

Color displays require periodic adjustment to maintain the proper registration of images. Otherwise, characters formed by a combination of primary colors (pink, yellow, turquoise, and white) may appear as characters in each of the component primary colors. For example, pink characters may appear red with blue shadows.

Unless the display has self-adjusted registration or a simple user adjustment control, use mixed colors conservatively. If the display has user adjustable registration, novice users should be made aware of the color adjustment procedure early in their training. Problems of registration are more common near the corners and edges of displays. Registration problems do not occur when characters are displayed in a single primary color (red, green, or blue). *Robertson, 1980*

Assigning Colors for Coding

In selecting specific colors to be used for specific purposes, the human-computer interface designer can benefit from guidelines to avoid some common pitfalls. The assignment of colors should be based on legibility, consistency, meaningfulness, and the characteristics of the display device.

Some general guidelines are listed below, but these should not be interpreted as universal rules. The generally recommended color assignments may be inappropriate for a given display device because of its limitations or eccentricities in color or brightness. Prevailing color use conventions in a given user population may take precedence over general recommendations. The prudent designer should develop a tentative color assignment scheme and try it out on the target display devices and users before finalizing it.

4.8 Definition of Code Colors
Define each color code.

When color is used for special coding, show the meaning of the code colors on the display . Use a given color for only one meaning on a display format. For example, if yellow is used to indicate data related to technology contracts, yellow should not be used for "caution" on the same screen. Display the label defining a code color in that color.

Example:
If red data indicate "overdue" and yellow data indicate "pending", the bottom line of the data display area should contain "red = overdue" in red, and "yellow = pending" in yellow.

Exception:
Color meanings which are consistently defined and used on all displays in the system may not require definition on every screen.

4.9 Consistency of Color Coding
Use color codes consistently.

Color coding must be as consistent as possible from screen to screen. Example: If data related to pending contracts are displayed in yellow on one screen, display them in yellow on all screens on which such data appear. If pending contracts data are arbitrarily in yellow on some screens and in other colors on other screens, the user's task of display interpretation will be more difficult. Not only are the potential advantages of color coding lost, but the display will be more difficult to interpret than a similar monochromatic display. *Galitz, 1981; Krebs, Wolf, and Sandvig, 1978.*

4.10 Abnormal Color Vision
Coding allows for color-weak users.

Variations in color may not be noticed by users with abnormal color perception, so critical information must not be presented by color code alone. (The term "abnormal color perception" is preferred over "color blindness" because most color-deficient people have trouble perceiving only certain colors. True lack of any color perception is extremely rare.) Approximately eight percent of the males in a user group may be expected to have weak or abnormal color perception. The proportion of female users having color perception abnormalities may be expected to be much smaller. *Durrett and Trezona, 1982; IBM, 1979, 1984; Robertson, 1980*

4.11 Color Meanings
Color code reflects common color meanings.

Color itself may convey information. The association of red with "stop", yellow with "caution", and green with "go" is strong, and these colors may be used in displays without having to teach the association to display users. If other meanings are assigned to these colors, the strength of the common meanings can lead to misinterpretation, though other associations with display colors may be taught. Choose color meanings commonly held in the population-at-large and meanings that already exist in the job.

See Table 4-1 for some data on the strength of certain color meanings. The table shows the percent of subjects *(Bergum and Bergum, 1981)* who associated certain colors with certain meanings. Red, yellow, green, and blue showed commonly held associations with specific meanings. Other colors showed less agreement among subjects.
Durrett and Trezona, 1982; Galitz, 1981.

Table 4-1.   Color Stereotypes (% Verbal Associations)

COLOR	MEANING	% ASSOCIATING COLOR & MEANING
Red	Stop	100%
	Hot	94%
	Danger	90%
Yellow	Caution	81%
Green	Go	99%
	Safe	61%
Blue	Cold	96%

(based on Bergum and Bergum, 1981)

4.12 Relevant Color Codes
Use task- relevant color coding.

Use color coding on display elements that are relevant to the user's task. The user will be distracted, rather than aided if color coding distinguishes among irrelevant categories.

Example:
Users may not need to concern themselves with whether their inquiries are processed by the operating system or automatically handled by some other utility. If this is the case, designers should not use color coding on this dimension (for example, displaying system outputs in blue and utility outputs in green). *Christ, 1975; Galitz, 1981*

4.13 Highlight Sparingly
Use color highlighting conservatively.

If color is used to highlight or emphasize particular fields, do not overuse it. As the number of highlighted items goes up, the effectiveness of the highlighting goes down. *Christ, 1975; Carter, 1979; Robertson, 1980*

4.14 Similar Colors
Use similar colors for related data.

Similar colors can be used to indicate similarities among data. Colors that tend to be perceived as similar include red-pink, yellow-orange, red-orange, blue-violet, and blue-turquoise.

Example:
Accounts that are 60 days overdue are displayed in red and those that are 30 days overdue are displayed in pink. *Galitz, 1981; Robertson, 1980*

4.15 Contrasting Colors
Use contrasting colors to distinguish data.

Contrasting colors can be used to distinguish and separate categories of data or ranges of values.

Examples:
Pairs of colors with high contrast to each other include: red-turquoise (or cyan), blue-yellow, and green-pink (or magenta). For three high contrast colors, use red-blue-green. Four colors that contrast well with each other are red-blue-green-white. *Robertson, 1980*

4.16 Background Color
Use contrasting background colors.

When displaying colored text on a colored background, choose high contrast background/foreground color pairs. In general, lighter colors should be displayed on darker backgrounds and vice versa.

Example:
Display yellow letters on a blue background, rather than a white background. *Durrett and Trezona, 1982; McTyre and Frommer, 1985; Pace, 1984*

4.17 Reverse Video Color
Use contrasting reverse video colors.

Some colors that are legible in "normal" video (colored characters on a black background) may not be as legible in reverse video (black characters on a colored background). In these cases legibility may be improved by defining the reverse video as a white character (rather than a black character) on a colored background, if the display system provides the capability to do so.

Recommended Color Code
4.18 Base Color
Use white or black as the base color.

Use white characters on a black background, or black characters on a
white background as the default or base color. Display data in colors
other than black or white only when the change of color will aid the user.
Additional colors should not be used simply to provide variety in the
appearance of screens or to make screens pretty. To do so may reduce
the effectiveness of color when it is used to convey information.

Exceptions:
On some display devices, extensive use of white, either as a background
or foreground color, may lead to excessive display brightness and visual
discomfort for users. Other devices may have color registration problems
(see 4.7) that may be reduced by minimizing the use of white. In these
cases, green may be a better choice for the base color. *Robertson, 1980*

74

4.19 Alarms
Display alarms in red.

Present data associated with alarms, errors, dangerous conditions, or
information requiring immediate attention in red. Display each input field
in which errors have been detected in red until its errors have been
corrected. If some users will work at monochromatic terminals or use
monochromatic hardcopy devices, data that are displayed in red on color
terminals to indicate a need for immediate attention must be highlighted
(for example, increased brightness) on monochromatic terminals.
MIL-STD-1472C, 1981

4.20 Hot
Use red to indicate a hot temperature.

Red has a strong association with heat, and thus makes a good color
code for indicating a hot temperature. For example, overheated
components or data representing overheated conditions could be
displayed in red. Heat controls could use red for "hotter" and blue for
"colder". *Bergum and Bergum, 1981*

4.21 Warnings
Display warnings in yellow.

Present data and messages associated with noncritical warnings, marginal conditions, or possible action requirements in yellow. *MIL-STD-1472C, 1981*

4.22 Normal Conditions
Use green to indicate normal conditions.

Green is an effective color for conveying status conditions that are normal or within acceptable tolerance range. *MIL-STD-1472C, 1981*

4.23 "Go"
Use green for go.

Green also has a strong association with "go" in modern societies due to the familiar traffic light. *Bergum and Bergum, 1981*

4.24 Use of Blue
Restrict saturated blue to background use.

Use blue for background, graphics, and low criticality items, but not for primary data. The blue usually used in displays has low contrast, and blue has inherent problems in visual focusing as well, especially for older observers. Important information normally should not be displayed in blue, though for shading areas in graphic displays and for de-emphasizing parts of a display, its low brightness may be beneficial.

Exception:
On display devices that give the designer extensive control over the hue and saturation of colors, the problems normally associated with highly saturated ("deep") blue can be reduced by using a desaturated ("light") blue or a mixed-color shade that is still recognized as blue. *Krebs, Wolf, Sandvig, 1978*

Color

4.25 Cold
Use blue to indicate cold or water.

If the legibility problems associated with blue (see 4.24) can be overcome by judicious selection of the shade of blue, the color blue can be used to indicate a cold temperature. Because of its common use on maps, blue is also a good color for indicating water, particularly bodies of water on a map. *Bergum and Bergum, 1981*

4.26 Additional Color Coding
Use color for differentiation.

If it is necessary to use several colors to differentiate, call out, or group data on a screen, colors may be applied in ways other than those described in previous paragraphs. The colors without strongly associated meanings, such as turquoise, white and pink, may be used to differentiate particular groups or displayed data that have a common feature or those that require categorizing or particular attention. Table 4-2 provides a summary of the recommended uses of specific colors. *Brown et al., 1980, 1983; Cakir, Hart, and Stewart, 1980*

Table 4-2.
Summary of Color Coding Recommendations

COLOR	USE
White/Black	Base color
Red	Alarms or errors; Stop
Yellow	Warnings or data that may require attention
Green	Normal or OK; Go; Base color if white is too bright.
Saturated Blue	De-emphasis, shading; Not for critical data
Desaturated Blue	Cold temperature or water
Pink (Magenta)	Secondary alarm color, differentiating data
Turquoise (Cyan)	Differentiating data types
Other Colors	Differentiating data types

4.27 Color Graphics
Use color for graphics.

Color is particularly well suited for use in graphical displays. Color is more effective than varying fill patterns to distinguish the components of a chart. For pictorial graphics, color permits more flexibility and realism.

Examples:
Use different colors for each of the curves on a line graph, for each of the sections in a pie chart, or for each of the items in a bar chart. *Cakir, Hart, and Stewart, 1980; Stahr, 1984*

Note:
If the chart will subsequently be printed on a monochromatic printer, code items with varying fill patterns, line patterns, and so forth in addition to color.

Chapter Five
Graphics

As computer graphics hardware and software becomes more sophisticated, and at the same time cheaper and more readily available, graphics are finding widespread application in human-computer interface design. New user interface design approaches are using graphical and pictorial representation as an integral part of the dialogue, rather than as just an optional way of displaying data. Advances in computer technology will make capabilities that are prohibitively expensive or perhaps even nonexistent today become commonplace. Innovations in the use of graphics to display data more effectively and to enable more intuitive communication between humans and computers are almost certain to continue.

Perhaps the most important advantage offered by the appropriate use of graphical presentation is in increasing the rate at which a human can extract, process, understand, and respond to the relevant information from a display. This corresponds closely to the Fitts and Seeger (1953) definition of stimulus- response compatibility discussed in Chapter 1: " ... the ensemble of stimulus and response combinations comprising the task results in a high rate of information transfer." When the display is presented in a form that is most compatible with human information processing, the amount of perceptual and mental recoding required to use the displayed data is minimized. The transfer of information is faster, errors are less likely, and less training and practice are required for mastery.

Two important ways in which graphics can enhance information transfer rates are:

1   by presenting objects in a pictorial rather than verbal form, and

2   by presenting complex data in a form which permits visual comparisons of amounts, trends, and relationships.

Effective Uses of Graphics
For many types of data the picture is indeed worth a thousand words and the chart is worth a dozen tables of numbers. The human ability to extract information from visual scenes is much more fundamental than our ability to manipulate data verbally or arithmetically. *Carlson, 1976; Schmid and Schmid, 1979; Schwartz and Howell, 1985*

5.1 Reducing Display Density
Use graphics to reduce display density.

Graphical presentation often permits the designer to present a large
amount of data in a simple, succinct, and easily interpreted form.
Relationships among several variables may require hundreds of numbers
in a table in an alphanumeric data format. The same relationships may be
effectively presented in a single, simple chart in graphical format. (See
Figure 5.1.)

Tabular Presentation

Production	Plant A Quality	Plant B Quality	Plant C Quality
1000	90%	85%	95%
3000	92%	78%	55%
5000	88%	62%	37%
7000	95%	48%	27%
9000	88%	42%	21%

Graphical Presentation

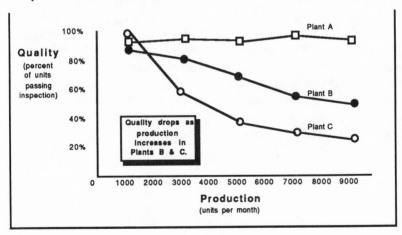

Figure 5.1 Comparison of Tabular and Graphical Presentation.

5.2 Mimic Displays
Use graphics to show component relationships.

A mimic display is a schematic representation of the relationships among the physical components of a system. For example, some cars have a dashboard display showing a small line drawing of a car. When an alarm occurs, such as "Door Ajar", the alarm is displayed at the appropriate location on the drawing (in this case at the location of the unclosed door).

In more complex systems, the mimic display can be especially effective in

1   providing a context for the users' decisions,

2   providing a readily interpretable summary of the status of the system and its components, and

3   providing a natural medium for the user to manipulate the components with direct representation of the system-wide impacts of each action. *Hinsley and Hanes, 1977*

5.3 Displaying Relationships
Use graphics to display complex relationships.

Graphical representations, such as bar charts and line charts, of the relationship between two or more variables, can often be much more effective than a table of numbers in communicating complex relationships among the variables. Extensive mental arithmetic may often be required to extract the salient conclusions from a table of numbers, and the user may overlook important conclusions completely. A properly constructed and labeled graph can often make complex relationships obvious from quick visual inspection. (See Figure 5.2.) *Hinsley and Hanes, 1977; Paller, Szoka, and Nelson, 1981*

Tabular Presentation

Accuracy	Model 1 Cost	Model 2 Cost
65%	$45	$110
70%	$65	$150
75%	$90	$220
80%	$110	$260
85%	$220	$280
90%	$350	$300
95%	$500	$320
99%	$1100	$350

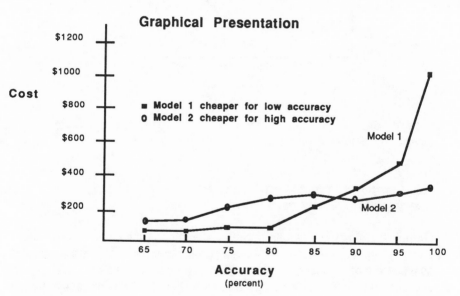

Figure 5.2
Graphical Presentation Facilitates Interpreting Relationships

5.4 Display of Trends
Use graphics to display trends.

Graphical displays can often aid in effective presentation of trends. For example, a chart showing the changes of one or more variables over time can make it much easier for a user to detect cyclical variations, project into the future, or interpolate between two intervals. Line charts are generally more effective than bar charts for displaying trends. (See Figure 5.3.) *McCormick, 1976; Swezey and Davis, 1983*

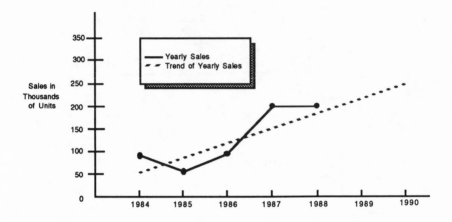

Figure 5.3
Graph to Show Trend

5.5 Comparison with Projections
Use graphics to display predicted vs. actual values.

Graphical plots of actual data (monthly sales) can be superimposed upon a plot of target or predicted data (sales goals) to provide an instant visual assessment of actual performance, deviation from projections, and overall trends. In most cases interpretation of such data is much simpler from a well designed graphical display than from a numerical or textual counterpart. Paller, Szoka, and Nelson (1981) have suggested that the graphs use solid lines for actual data and dotted or dashed lines for projected data. (See Figure 5.4.)

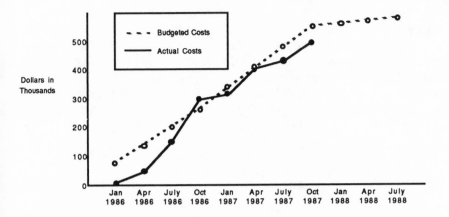

Figure 5.4
Graph to Compare Predicted vs. Actual Values

5.6 *Display of Limits*
Use graphics to display actual vs. limits of variables.

In user interfaces designed to monitor and control the performance of a system or machine, the actual performance of the system can be shown along with the safe limits or "nominal envelopes" of the appropriate variables for comparison. Graphics can be particularly effective in this situation. The user can not only track the current (and perhaps past) performance of the system, but can also visually evaluate the extent to which performance is within safe limits. The limits displayed may include:

1   marginal limits that define the levels at which caution should be applied ("condition yellow" limits),

2   critical limits that define the tolerance levels at which serious hazards exist ("condition red" limits), and

3   a plot of ideal or nominal limits for use as a goal. In systems with color capabilities, the limit lines or markers can be yellow for marginal limits and red for critical limits.

5.7 Exact readings
Avoid graphics for exact numeral readings.
Don't use graphical charts to display numerical values for which exact reading is required. While graphical charts permit quick visual comparisons of magnitudes, relationships, and trends, they are not well suited for reading exact values. Reading a specific value from a graph usually requires tracing a value back onto its axes, which is not only inaccurate, but also requires extra mental and perhaps physical steps such as tracing with a straight edge. When exact readings are required, present the numbers digitally with the appropriate level of accuracy.
Grether and Baker, 1972; Hinsley and Hanes, 1977

5.8 Rapidly Changing Data
Use graphics for dynamic data.

Use analog or graphical presentation for rapidly changing numeric values. A digital numeric display of a rapidly changing value may appear as a blur, changing too fast to be easily read by a user. An analog display (such as a meter), a computer-generated facsimile of an analog display, or an appropriately designed graphical chart (such as a bar chart) can permit easier monitoring of a rapidly changing display. For example, tachometer readings in an automobile change too rapidly to permit accurate reading of a digital display, so the tachometer should be an analog meter or graphical display. *Hinsley and Hanes,1977*

5.9 Map displays
Use map displays for geographical data.

Geographical data or data associated with a geographical frame of reference may be more easily interpreted when presented in a graphical map display format.

5.10 Interpolation
Use graphics for quick interpolation.

Graphical displays such as line charts facilitate interpolation between measured or actual values to intermediate values for which data is not available. When quick, approximate interpolation is required, an appropriate graph is preferred to a table of numbers.

Icons

Modern computer dialogues often incorporate graphical representations of the objects and actions available to the user. These representations are typically called icons. Icons are miniature images of objects such as file cabinets, file folders, sheets of paper, trash cans, and printers. Graphical representations of actions, cursors, programs, and other dialogue elements in addition to physical objects, are often called icons, as well.

Marcus (1984a) defines the term icon more restrictively than the common- usage definition. He makes distinctions among icons, indexes, and symbols. "An icon is something that looks like what it means; it is representational and easy to understand." An index is a sign that is caused by the thing to which it refers. A symbol is a sign that may be completely arbitrary in appearance; we must learn the association of its appearance with its meaning. In common usage, however, the term icon is often used to refer to all three kinds of signs.

5.11 Visual Interfaces

Icons facilitate direct manipulation.

In many human-computer interface designs, icons and symbols can be directly manipulated by the user in an analogous way to the actual objects they represent. If appropriately applied, visual interface techniques can permit simple conceptualization of the system's operations through common, real-world analogies. These techniques can help the user in maintaining context and orientation, as well as minimizing requirements for memorization of commands and syntax. (See Figure 5.5.) *Marcus, 1984(a), 1984(b); Shneiderman, 1983; Smith, Irby, Kimball, and Verplank, 1982; Woodmansee, 1983*

Graphics

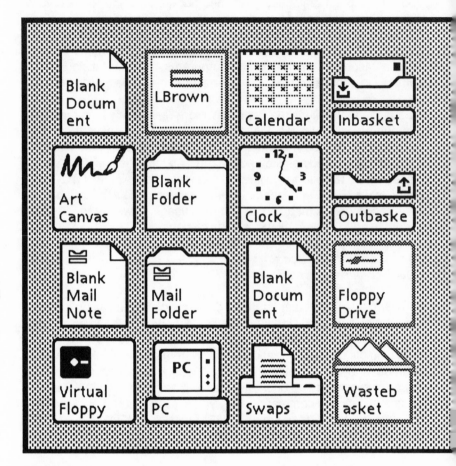

Figure 5.5
Example of Graphical Icons

5.12 Compact Representation
Icons can save space.

A graphical representation of an object, action, or concept can often be presented in a smaller area than an equivalent text label or description. This can permit the user to access more information in a limited display space. A well-designed icon can sometimes clearly convey a meaning in the equivalent of a few character positions, when that meaning might take several paragraphs to convey in text. The appropriate icon may be easier to recognize and comprehend than any amount of text. *Marcus, 1984(a)*

Example:

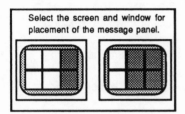

Select the screen and window for placement of the message panel.	**Window Selection Icon**

```
Select the screen and window for
placement of the message panel.

Screen: __      Row: __
1. Left         1. Top
2. Right        2. Bottom

                Column: __
                1. Left
                2. Center
                3. Right
```

Window Selection Menu

5.13 International Symbols
Icons can permit international use.

Properly designed icons can reduce the reliance of the human-computer interface upon a single national language. When a system must be used by people of different nationalities who speak different languages, the use of icons can reduce some of the language barrier problems. Icons can permit international communication for computer users analogous to international highway signs for drivers. *Marcus, 1984(a), Tognazzini, 1985*

Graphics

5.14 Legible Icons
Design icons for legibility.

Design icons carefully to ensure that they are legible. Consider the characteristics of the display device(s) in developing the graphical design. A high resolution device can permit more detailed elements to be incorporated into the icon. Lower resolution devices may require that icons be simpler or larger to ensure that the icon can be reliably identified at a normal viewing distance. *Marcus, 1984(a)*

5.15 Use Clear Icons
Use icons that represent their meanings clearly.

Well designed icons are self-explanatory, at least within the context in which they are used. There are several tips for designing clear icons:

1 use concrete representations of actual objects or actions,

2 emphasize the graphical elements that distinguish this object from other objects,

3 simplify the representation by eliminating or de-emphasizing the elements that don't contribute to the object's identification, and

4 follow consistent design conventions in constructing all the icons in the system, such as the use, appearance, and location of text labels, borders, and other elements embedded into the icon.

Example:
One keyboard design uses extensive graphical labeling of keys. The print key is labelled with the icon shown in the "DON'T USE" example below. This symbol produces little or no association with printers or printouts. Simply labelling the key with the word "PRINT" would make the key's function obvious. If an international label were required, the icon in the "USE" example, a facsimile of a printer, would convey the meaning effectively.

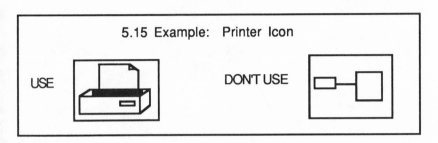

5.15 Example: Printer Icon

USE   DON'T USE

5.16 Inappropriate Use of Icons
Avoid the use of confusing icons.

Just as some concepts are more easily represented pictorially than in words, many others are much more naturally presented in words than pictures. Icons cannot completely replace words in any but the simplest user interfaces. Use icons for concepts that can be represented clearly with graphics, but do not try to force icons to fit every user interface need. For some applications, other techniques may be more appropriate than icons. *Marcus, 1984(a)*

Example:
Whiteside, Jones, Levy, and Wixon (1985) compared user performance on a file manipulation task using several different commercial computer operating systems. Some of the operating systems were command-based, some were menu-based, and some were icon-based. Their results showed poorer performance using these particular icon-based systems than using these particular command or menu systems on this particular task.

Graphics

Chapter Six
Dialogue Design

One of the most critical determinants of user satisfaction and acceptance of a computer system is the extent to which the user feels in control of an interactive session. If users cannot control the direction and pace of the dialogue, they are likely to feel frustrated, intimidated, or threatened by the computer system. Their productivity may suffer, or they may avoid using the system at all.

The extent of system control perceived by the user depends significantly on the extent to which information is provided. This information can make an otherwise difficult and time-consuming task easy and fast. The following guidelines present principles and techniques to make the user's tasks easier.

Status Information
Provide evidence of system status at all times. After an entry, the users need feedback to know whether the system is down, in a loop, in some other error mode, or just in the midst of processing the input. When processing time of a given input is long, feedback on the status of the request is particularly important. *Galitz, 1980*

6.1 Intermediate Feedback
Provide input acknowledgement and progress indicators.

Provide intermediate feedback that acknowledges acceptance of the input and indicates that the system is waiting for processing to be completed. Delays longer than a few seconds can be troublesome for some users unless an indication is given that the system is working. A message such as "Please wait while the system processes your request" may be acceptable. However, provide a dynamic progress indicator whenever it is feasible (Myers, 1985). Dynamic indicators provide feedback on how long the wait may be, give feedback that the processing is continuing smoothly, and hold the user's interest during the wait. *Engel and Granda, 1975; Frey, Sides, Hunt, and Rouse, 1983; Myers, 1985*

Examples:

1   A numeric or graphical percent-done progress indicator provides not only feedback that the request has been accepted, but also an indication of how much waiting remains. For example, a graphical image of a gauge or meter that reads from 0 to 100 percent could

display percent-done. On a system without graphical capabilities, numeric percent-done indicators could be used.

2   A counter can provide feedback on how many of a series of operations have been completed. For example, a print routine could show the page number of the page now printing, such as "Now printing page number N", where N represents the current page number.

3   In many situations a count-down counter is preferable to a count-up counter as in the example above. A count-down counter shows the number of operations remaining to be performed, which is often a better indication of the time to completion than the number of operations completed. For example, in a file copying program, the progress indicator could be "N more files to copy".

4   When the number of operations is not excessive, the computer could list each operation as it is performed. For example, in a file copying program, the computer could list each file as it is copied:
    "Chapter 1" file successfully copied.
    "Chapter 2" file successfully copied.
    "Chapter 3" file successfully copied.

6.2 Input acknowledgement
Acknowledge successful completion.

Acknowledge the execution of an input. When processing of a request is completed, some feedback should be given. Often this feedback is implicit in the displaying of the requested data, but when successful execution does not cause any change in the display, a PROCESSING SUCCESSFULLY COMPLETED message should be added. *Engel and Granda, 1975*

6.3 Blank Screen
Do not leave the screen blank.

Always give the user an indication of how to continue. A user left viewing a blank screen has no indication of how to continue, what mode the system is in, or even whether the system is working. *Peterson, 1979.*

6.4 Mode Designator
Display mode indicators.

When the system is operating in a special mode for which a different set of commands or syntax rules are in effect, provide users with an indicator that distinguishes this mode from other modes. Provide differences in headings, formats, or prompts, and use labels to remind the user of the mode that is in effect. For example, the edit mode can be distinguished from the command mode by the presence of a characteristic header or distinctly different screen format and the word EDIT prominently displayed on the screen. *Elam, 1980.*

6.5 Transaction Type
Display the current transaction type.

Display the transaction category name of the current transaction. Within the same mode there may be categories of transactions that serve very different kinds of functions. For example, a data base application may have separate transaction categories for reports, adding data, changing data, deleting data, menu screens to select other transactions, and HELP screens for online assistance. Displaying the category name (REPORT, ADD, CHANGE, DELETE, MENU, or HELP) prominently on the screen helps the user to maintain a frame of reference.

6.6 System Entry
Explain down time.

If a user will not be able to get onto the system, send a message telling why and approximately when the problem is expected to be corrected. For example, display SYSTEM DOWN FOR MAINTENANCE UNTIL 9:30 AM. Avoid "as soon as possible" messages; make an estimate and update it as required. *Brown et al., 1980, 1983*

6.7 Explicit Options
Display available options.

Rather than requiring users to remember which options are available at each step in the dialogue, display a list of the currently active options. Temporarily inactive options (those that are not applicable in the current stage of the dialogue) may also be displayed if their inactive status is shown. *Brown et al., 1980,1983; Elam, 1980; Peterson, 1979*

6.8 Memory Requirements
Display needed information.

Do not require the user to remember information not displayed on the current screen. The user must not have to decide what action to take from memory. inaccuracies of memory will lead to errors and lost time. *Brown et al., 1980, 1983; Engel and Granda, 1975*

6.9 Sequence Continuation
Displays indicate how to continue.

Indicate on each screen the user response that is necessary to continue the interaction sequence. Do not leave the user viewing a screen with no indication of how to continue.

USE   DON'T USE

Data Base Status
Data is current through
March 1985
To continue, Enter NEXT ID or press PF 11.

Data Base Status
Data is current through
March 1985.

Brown et al., 1980, 1983; Engel and Granda, 1975

6.10 Multi-screen Transactions
Place frequently used steps first.

For transactions requiring multiple screens, locate the most frequently requested data on the earliest screens. Allow users to skip later screens in the sequence if this is reasonable in the transaction. *Galitz, 1981*

6.11 Visible Effects
What you see is what you get.

The results of user entries and actions should be directly and accurately portrayed on the display.

Example:
A word processing program should enable the user to view on the screen exactly what the pages will look like when printed. Users find it very difficult to ensure that proper spacing, margins, page breaks, and alignment have been achieved unless they can view an exact rendition of the printed page before printing. If this is not possible in the input mode, the program should provide a "FORMAT CHECK" mode. This mode incorporates the requested margins and tabs and shows what the printout will look like with all non–printing characters and embedded commands removed. *Smith et. al., 1982.*

6.12 Access to Settings
What you see is what you've got.

Provide ways for the user to easily determine the settings of all dialogue parameters. For example, in a word processing application, the user should be able to quickly determine the settings of parameters such as line spacing, character size and font, margins, and tabs. *Shneiderman, 1986*

6.13 Reversible Actions
Provide an "UNDO" function.

Provide the capability to recover from unwanted or incorrect actions. An "UNDO" function, which reverses the effect of the last action taken, is often used to provide this capability. The ability to immediately recover from an inadvertent or erroneous action (or an action with different results than expected) has several advantages for users:

1   It can eliminate the necessity to reinitiate a whole series of transactions that led to the previous step in the dialogue.

2   One can recover from mistakes that might otherwise have led to the destruction of data, requiring reentry or perhaps permanent loss of those data .

3   It can minimize users' fear of getting into a situation from which they do not know how to return.

4   By trial–and–error exploration, users can learn the system or expand their knowledge to functions they have not previously used .

Example:
The user is not sure which of the titles shown on a selection list performs the desired function. He chooses the one that seems most likely, but the result is not what was he wanted, and his original data have been modified. The UNDO function permits him to reverse the last transaction and thus avoid having to reenter or reconstruct his original data.

Note:
The need for reversible actions applies at many levels, from the ability to back up with cursor control or tabbing keys to the need in some applications to retrieve the previous version of a file. Actual inverse functions (such as "tab left" and "tab right") tend to be more natural and more easily understood than UNDO (for those functions for which an inverse exists). *Foley and Wallace, 1974; Galitz, 1980; Shneiderman, 1982b; Smith et al., 1982*

Menus
A menu is a list of options from which a selection or selections can be made by the user. It provides to the user an explicit list of available options, permitting selection by recognition rather than requiring recall. Menus provide a useful technique to make computer systems more accessible to novice users, less demanding on the memory of infrequent users, and , if properly designed, more efficient even for experienced users. If not carefully designed to accommodate both experienced and novice users, however, menu dialogues can be intolerably slow and frustrating for expert users. *Perlman, 1984*

Modern dialogue designs have expanded the definition, responsiveness, and functionality of menus considerably over traditional menu techniques. Traditionally, menus were full-screen text lists of options. The user was required to work step by step through a hierarchical series of menu screens with (typically) a long response time between each selection. Advancements in display technology, computer memory, local intelligence, graphics, and user interface innovations have permitted menus to be much more flexible and efficient. Menu windows, pop-up and pull-down menus, graphical and iconic menus, and nearly

Dialogue Design

instantaneous menu response time have become commonplace. Many of the traditional objections to menu systems for experienced users need not apply.

6.14 Main Menu
Make the menu easily accessible.

When using a menu system, provide rapid access to the main menu at all times. The user should not have to backtrack to return to the starting level in a hierarchical menu system. This capability can be provided by dedicating a program function key, a light pen or touch field, or a cursor entry field to display the main menu.
Brown et al., 1980, 1983

6.15 Multiple Paths
Provide menu bypass capability.

Permit the user to request displays or options from non–menu screens and from menus not showing the desired selection. Menus are helpful for novices to the system or to a part of the system, but working step–by–step through several levels of a menu hierarchy is slow and unnecessary for experienced users. *Galitz, 1981*

Examples: Direct routing techniques include:

1 command language entries,

2 macros (sequences of commands or actions initiated by a single input),

3 "stacking" menu requests, and

4 typing the memorized number, name, or ID or the desired display.

6.16 Entry Stacking
Allow type-ahead entry stacking.

When possible, permit stacking of inputs or multiple entries. When experienced users are responding to the first of a sequence of selection screens and know before seeing them how they will respond to the next several screens, they should be able to input several entries at the same time. Sequential entries can be separated by a special character; a semicolon is recommended. For example,

COST CATEGORIES.

```
CODE                          CATEGORY

L                             Labor
M                             Material

Enter selected code: L R T
```

(The R and T entry codes are normally displayed as selections at the next two menu levels, but three entries can be made simultaneously by users who have memorized the desired codes. The two intermediate menus are thus bypassed.) *Engel and Granda, 1975; Shneiderman,1983a*

6.17 Menu Wording
Use clear wording of menu selections.

Spell out the selection options on a menu list. Choose words that make the function of each option clear and distinct from the other options. Minimize the use of abbreviations in menu items.

6.18 Consistent Titles
Make screen titles consistent with menu wording.

Use the same title for an option in a menu listing as the screen title of that selection. Users will expect to see the same words that they selected from the menu when the selected screen appears. A different screen title may lead them to believe that they made a selection error.

6.19 Menu Order
List menu items in appropriate order.

Menu items can be listed by several different ordering schemes. The appropriate ordering scheme depends on the nature of the items and their typical uses, but a systematic ordering technique should be applied. Possible orders include the following:

1 chronological
   (time ordered),

2 numerical
   (listed by size or quantity),

3 alphabetical
   (alphabetical order of item names),

4 sequential
   (listed by typical sequence of use),

5 functional
   (functionally related items listed together),

6 importance
   (most critical items listed first), and

7 frequency
   (most often used items listed first).

Brown et al., 1980,1983

6.20 Inactive Menu Options
Display only active menu options.

When designing selection menus, do not include options that are planned, but not yet implemented. Unimplemented options clutter the screen and may send the user down dead-end transaction paths. *Smith and Aucella, 1983.*

Example:
When the "Inventory Data Base" is planned for future implementation, but is not online, don't display its name on the main menu.

USE

```
ID = MM                        MAIN MENU                      Page 1 of 1

Enter the selected Data Base ID as the NEXT ID.

ID   DATA BASE NAME

M    Manufacturing Data Base
A    Accounting Data Base
S    Scheduling Data Base

NEXT ID: _ _ _
```

DON'T USE

```
ID =MM                         MAIN MENU                      Page 1 of 1
Enter the selected Data Base ID as the NEXT ID.

ID   DATA BASE NAME

M  Manufacturing Data Base
A  Accounting Data Base
S  Scheduling Data Base
I   Inventory Data Base

NEXT ID: _ _ _
```

Exceptions:
Some systems display options that are momentarily inappropriate at the current stage of the dialogue in shaded characters while displaying currently active options in normal characters. This technique is valuable in providing the user with a consistent, familiar menu selection list, yet designating when some of the options are momentarily unavailable or inapplicable in the current situation.

Dialogue Design

Example:
The figure below is a menu of File options. "New" and "Open..." are implemented options, but are not appropriate in the current situation.

Soft Machine Controls

Nakatani and Rohrlich (1983) have described a "soft machine" philosophy for designing user dialogues with computer systems. A soft machine is a software-driven emulation of a hardware display/control device, such as a panel of pushbuttons, indicator lights, knobs, dials, or meters. The "hard machine" display is emulated by a CRT or plasma panel facsimile and the control activation is emulated by a cursor control selection device or by a touch sensitive overlay.

Hard machines (conventional stoves, toasters, stereos) have some ease-of-use advantages over traditional computer interfaces such as command languages. They are simpler and more intuitive to use. Their functions are usually mapped one-on-one with their controls. Their appearance thus gives an indication of how they are operated. However, they also tend to be inflexible, difficult or impossible to reconfigure to support new functions, and limited in the number of functions they can support in comparison with the open functionality of computers.
By emulating hard machines in a software-controlled, reconfigurable medium, soft machines can capture the benefits of both hard machines (for ease and naturalness of use) and computer systems (for flexibility, functionality, and ease of reconfiguration). A soft machine interface can

emulate a large number of different hard machines on the same physical device, and can be reconfigured in seconds to replace a module that is not currently required. *Nakatani and Rohrlich, 1983; Seminara and Eckert, 1980*

Tognazzini (1985) has described several kinds of soft controls with recommendations for their use: buttons, check boxes, radio buttons, and dials. All of these techniques, which will be described in the following sections, use a pointing and selecting device to perform direct, cause-and-effect manipulation on graphical objects and their labels.

6.21 Soft Machine Menus
Consider presenting menus as soft controls.

Menus are often a good application of the soft machine philosophy. Options can be presented as graphical facsimiles of labelled pushbuttons or checklists. A cursor pointing and selection device, such as a mouse or light pen, or a touch sensitive overlay is used to "push" the selected button.

6.22 Buttons
Use soft buttons to initiate actions.

Soft buttons are small displayed objects, such as boxes or facsimiles of pushbuttons, labelled with text. Pointing and clicking on the button (with a mouse) or touching the button (with a finger on a touchscreen) initiates the action indicated by the button's label instantly after pressing. Buttons are typically used to permit the user to select among a small number of options (typically about two to five) to be activated immediately after the button press. Example of functions for which buttons are commonly used include acknowledging messages and cancelling or proceeding with actions which require confirmation (such as deleting a file). *Tognazzini, 1985*

Example:
The "Done" and "Cancel" buttons in Figure 6.1 are examples of this type of soft control. They are used by a document processing program to close the Table Properties window shown in the figure. "Done" causes the new configuration to take effect, while "Cancel" returns to the previous configuration.

TABLE PROPERTIES				
Done	Apply	Cancel	Defaults	Reset

DISPLAY	FRAME	TABLE	HEADER	SORT KEYS

Margins	Left	0	Right	
	Top	.5	Bottom	
Captions	LEFT	RIGHT	TOP	BOTTOM
Width		7.35	FIXED	VARYING
Height		6.06	FIXED	VARYING
Alignment	FLUSH LEFT	CENTERED	FLUSH RIGHT	

Figure 6.1
"Table Properties" Window - Example of Various Soft Machine Controls.

6.23 State Boxes
Use state boxes to turn options on and off.

A state box, also called a check box, is a labelled box that controls the ON or OFF state of a parameter. By touching or clicking the state box with a cursor control device, the user can change the state of that parameter.State boxes show the current state of each parameter, typically by highlighting those that are ON or placing a mark beside them.

A series of state boxes can be presented in the same "menu", permitting the user to configure the whole cluster of related parameters at the same time. Unlike buttons, state boxes do not have an immediate effect. Instead, when the user signals that configuration is complete (often by a "Done" or "Enter" soft button), the reconfigured set of parameters take effect. *Tognazzini, 1985*

Example:
The items in Figure 6.1 under "Captions" are state boxes. The user can turn any combination of these caption location options ON or OFF by simply clicking on any box to change its state. Options that are ON are displayed in highlighted boxes; those that are OFF are displayed in unhighlighted boxes.

6.24 Choice Boxes
Use choice boxes for mutually exclusive choices.

Choice boxes (also called radio buttons after the station pre-set buttons on a car radio) are used to select among two or more mutually exclusive options. When one of a set of options is selected, the previously active option is automatically de-selected (like the car radio station pre-set buttons). Choice options are displayed as connected boxes to differentiate them from state options, which are displayed as unconnected boxes. *Tognazzini, 1985*

Example:
In Figure 6.1 the options under "Alignment" are choice boxes. The highlighted "CENTERED" option indicates that "CENTERED" is the currently selected option. Only one of these three alignments (FLUSH LEFT, CENTERED, or FLUSH RIGHT) can be in effect for a given table. Thus, if "FLUSH RIGHT" were selected, "CENTERED" would automatically be de-selected.

6.25 Soft Dials
Use soft dials for magnitude or position controls.

Soft machine techniques can also be used to emulate quantitative physical control/display devices, such as dials and meters. For example, some computer systems use a "scroll bar" to provide a technique for displaying and controlling the vertical or horizontal position in a file or on a virtual page. *Tognazzini, 1985*

Dialogue Design

Example:

Figure 6.2 shows several controls which are operated by moving an indicator directly using a cursor control device.

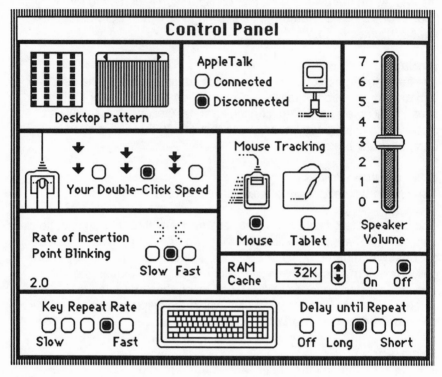

Figure 6.2.
Macintosh "Control Panel" Example of Various Soft Dials

6.26 Combined Controls
Use combinations of soft controls together.

In many human-computer interface design situations, soft control techniques such as those described above can be combined in the same window or transaction. This allows greater flexibility and permits setting or changing the configuration of parameters more quickly and easily, and in fewer transactions, than is typically possible using traditional menu systems.

Example:
Figure 6.1 shows a combination of buttons, state boxes, choice boxes, and dials used to completely configure an array of character format options in the same window with one transaction.

6.27 Soft Control Conventions
Conventions differentiate among soft control types.

Use different display conventions to discriminate among different types of soft controls. These will cue the user on whether a given option is an immediate-execute (button), a delayed-execute with multiple independent choices (state boxes), or a delayed-execute with mutually exclusive choices (choice boxes). A display convention for each should be established and observed consistently throughout the system.

Example:
In Figure 6.1 immediate action buttons are round-cornered rectangles inside the header. The choice boxes are connected boxes that use highlighting to indicate which mutually exclusive option is in effect. The state boxes are separated boxes that use highlighting to indicate "ON".

Commands
Command languages permit the user to control the computer dialogue by entering instructions to the computer, traditionally as type-in words, codes, or abbreviations. Modern dialogues often present command options on the display and permit the user to enter a command by pointing to its displayed label. These techniques have made the distinction between a command language and a menu system somewhat blurry. This section will focus primarily on dialogues that require the user to type memorized words, abbreviations, or codes, although alternatives will be mentioned.

A command language is often distinguished from a programming language by its immediately responsive, interactive nature. The programmer composes a long list of computer instructions for later compilation and execution. The command language user's instructions are carried out individually as the user enters them.

Command dialogues usually require extensive memorization of command names, arguments, and syntax. This can create problems for novices and intermittent users, but may be managed easily by expert frequent users. For experts, commands can offer short cuts, access to deeper levels of the system's functionality, and custom-tailoring of the dialogue. The challenge for human-computer interface designers is to identify and incorporate command naming, syntax, selection, and entry strategies that make the system easier to learn for novices and easier to use for both novices and experts.

6.28 Misspelling
Recognize common misspellings of commands.

When possible, a system should recognize common misspellings of a command and display a message showing the user the correct command. By confirming this message, the user can execute the command. If the user does not want to execute the system's corrected command, he or she can cancel rather than confirm. *Hayes, Ball, and Reddy,1981*

6.29 Similar Commands
Misspelling does not cause unintended actions.

Though the system should be tolerant of common misspellings, spelling errors should not produce valid system commands or initiate processing sequences different from those intended. Consider possible confusions with existing commands when selecting new command words. *Brown et al., 1983; Galitz, 1981; Shneiderman, 1979*

Example:

TO MEAN	USE	DON'T USE
Define a new procedure	PROCEDURE	PROCEDE
Calculate the difference (gross minus costs)	PROFIT	PROCEED

TO MEAN	USE	DON'T USE
Show insurance policy value	INS	INS
Ensure that forms are completed	CHECK	ENS

6.30 Truncated Commands
Allow truncation of commands.

Permit abbreviation of inputted commands. The system should recognize a command from the first one, two, or three letters (as necessary to make it distinct from other commands). Novice users can type in the entire command, while experienced users can abbreviate or truncate it. The system should accept either form. For example, if a P uniquely identifies a print command (no other commands start with P), it should be the user's option to enter either PRINT, PR, P, or any other truncation to initiate a print command. *Ehrenreich 1981, 1985*

6.31 Abbreviation Rules
Use consistent abbreviation rules for commands.

Follow a rule or set of rules for selecting command abbreviations. Truncation rules have been recommended by Ehrenreich (1981), but Grudin and Barnard (1984, 1985) suggest that the best abbreviation strategy may depend on whether the user is trying to construct the correct abbreviation from the word (encoding) or trying to reconstruct a word from the abbreviation (decoding) . Encoding is required to use abbreviations as type-in commands. Decoding is required to interpret abbreviated labels or data on a display.

In a subsequent survey of abbreviation experiments, Ehrenreich (1985) concluded that encoding an abbreviation is easier when a simple abbreviation rule is followed and taught to the user. Truncation has consistently proven to be the abbreviation rule of choice for encoding (remembering the abbreviation given the word). Decoding (remembering what a given abbreviation stands for), however, has not shown a consistent advantage for truncation rules (Rogers and Moeller, 1984). For example, "ACCO" may be the best type-in command abbreviation for "account" if truncated abbreviations are used for all commands. However, "ACCT" may be a better displayed label abbreviation to identify a data field.

Dialogue Design

6.32 Irreversible Commands
Require confirmation of destructive commands.

Require the user to confirm before executing a command that would result in extensive, irreversible changes. When feasible, the message requesting confirmation should provide a specific advisory about the irreversible consequences. For example, if the user enters a LOGOFF command before saving the data file he or she has created, a message such as "Your data will be lost if you logoff now. Do you want to save the file before logoff? (Y=yes, N=no, C=cancel command)".

6.33 Command Location
Use a consistent screen location for command entry.

When using commands in a formatted screen or window display, provide a command line(s) or field(s) in a consistent location on the screen or window. Granda et al. (1982) found that locating the command line near the bottom of the screen resulted in shorter command entry times than when the command line was located at the top of the screen. The number and magnitude of head movements was also less when commands were entered at the bottom, suggesting the potential for reducing the muscular fatigue sometimes associated with prolonged display terminal use. *Granda, Teitelbaum, and Dunlap, 1982; MIL-STD-1472C, 1981*

6.34 Command Consistency
Use consistent command syntax, arguments, and grammar.

Develop and follow consistent conventions for:

1 command syntax (the rules by which commands and their arguments are entered),

2 arguments (command extensions or qualifiers), and

3 grammar (the noun/verb, singular/plural, conventions used in commands).

Consistency reduces the memory load and uncertainty in recalling commands by presenting a familiar, predictable pattern. *Shneiderman, 1986*

Example:
Use a consistent syntax in the way that commands and their objects are connected.

USE   DON'T USE

| COPY 5 TO 15 | | COPY 5 TO 15 |
| DELETE 5 TO 15 | | DELETE 5:15 |

6.35   Command Syntax
Use command first, object second syntax.

For commands that specify an action (verb) and an object on which that action is to be performed, the syntax should be verb first, object second.

USE   DON'T USE

| INSERT TEXT | | INSERT TEXT |
| MOVE CURSOR | | CURSOR MOVE |

Exception:
In point-to-select dialogues, it may be preferable to select the object first, then the action to be performed on that object. *Shneiderman, 1986*

6.36 Hierarchical Commands
Use hierarchical command structures where applicable.

For systems with a large number of operations that are hierarchically related, or that can be specified by combining a selection from each of several independent categories, command hierarchies can minimize the number of command words to be memorized. For example, an action-object-destination hierarchy permits the user to specify a massive number of possible outcomes using only a few action names, a few object names, and a few destination names.

6.37 Congruent Commands
Use congruent command pairs.

For operations that have inverses or other counterparts, such as opening or closing a file, requesting the previous page or the next page, or inserting and deleting data, use congruent pairs of commands. Congruent pairs are usually formed from opposites or inverses.

USE

DON'T USE

READ/WRITE
OPEN/CLOSE
UP/DOWN
YES/NO

READ/CLOSE
OPEN/SAVE
PREVIOUS/DOWN
YES/OFF

6.38 Distinctive Commands

Choose distinctive, specific words for commands.

Commands that are distinctive, infrequently encountered, and specific words are more easily remembered than general and frequently used words. The word chosen for a command operation should discriminate that operation sharply from alternative interpretations or related operations. Less common words are also easier to associate with an operation because there are usually fewer competing associations for uncommon words.

USE

DON'T USE

INSERT
DELETE

ADD
REMOVE

Barnard, Hammond, MacLean, and Morton, 1982; Black and Moran, 1982; MIL-STD-1472C, 1981

6.39 Command Menus
Consider using command menus.

Pop-up or pull-down command menus offer an alternative to typed-in commands that makes the options explicit and requires no typing. These menus can be continually accessible, yet take up minimal screen space when not in use. Providing both command menus and type-in command counterparts supports novices, intermittent users, and experts. This multiple path approach also encourages the graceful evolution of a user from novice to expert. *MIL-STD-1472C, 1981*

6.40 Command Macros
Permit user- defined command sequences.

Macros are user-defined sequences of several commands that can be named, saved, and subsequently executed as a higher order command by simply entering the macro name. This capability is a valuable short-cut for experienced users and those who perform routine or repetitive operations.

6.41 Command Help
Provide access to command prompts.

Provide for prompts or HELP routines to show lists and definitions of valid commands, their valid arguments, and their syntax. *MIL-STD-1472C, 1981*

6.42 Command Punctuation
Minimize special characters in commands.

Use a minimum of punctuation and special characters in commands, especially those used in unfamiliar ways (other than standard punctuation). Keywords are often easier to understand and remember than special characters. If single letter abbreviations of the keywords are permitted, there may be no more key strokes required by the keyword approach than by special characters. *MIL-STD-1472C, 1981; Shneiderman, 1986*

System Response Time
System response time has been the object of considerable concern and attention, numerous studies and experiments, and varying recommendations for optimal response times. Adequate system response time is critical to user performance, accuracy, productivity, and satisfaction with the computer system. Response time requirements can also be major drivers of the cost of a computer system, so tradeoffs are usually required to develop a cost effective system.

For all its importance and the attention it has received, response time has proven to be one of the toughest categories for developing defensible guidelines. In fact the most common recommendations for optimal system response times today are derived from Miller's (1968) introspective analysis. Miller developed his recommendations by extrapolating from the maximum delays people find acceptable in conversations with other people.

Because the "optimal" response time may vary with the user's task, the dialogue used, the skill of the user, the user's expectations about what response time should be, and a host of other factors, simple universal answers to the question, "What should the maximum system response time be?" have not been forthcoming. The guidelines to follow, especially those that mention specific times, should be considered as general guidance to be qualified by task-specific, system-specific, and user-specific considerations.

116   A key factor determining acceptable response delays is level of closure. Delays that occur after the user has completed a planned sequence of actions are less disruptive than those that occur in the middle of a sequence. A delay after completing a major unit of work may not bother a user nor adversely affect performance. Delays between minor steps in a larger unit of work, however, may cause the user to forget the next planned steps. In general, actions with high levels of closure, such as saving a completed document to a file, are less sensitive to response time delays. Actions at the lowest levels of closure, such as typing a character and seeing it echoed on the display, are most sensitive to response time delays.

User response time, often called think time, is the interval between the presentation of information on a display and the user's next response. System response time affects user response time in several ways:

1   Delays of longer than a few seconds can result in the disruption of thought and short term memory for the next planned action(s).

2   When users expect long delays, they will take more time to organize and check their responses before entry, because the time cost to correct an error is high.

3 Conversely, when response time is very fast, users will respond quickly, not afraid to risk an error because an error can be quickly corrected.

4 System delays can reduce user response time under some circumstances, if the users plan and organize their next response during the waiting time.

Table 6.1 summarizes the response time criteria from MIL-STD-1472C (1981). These criteria are shown here with the same caveat MIL-STD-1472C gives:

System response time is highly application dependent. Therefore, the response times stated in this section are intended to be guidelines. Real-time systems (e.g., fire control systems, command and control systems) may require system response times more stringent than the guidelines, whereas, non-real-time systems may be designed with relaxed response times. MIL-STD-1472C, 1981

Table 6.1
Response Time Recommendations of MIL-STD-1472C

Action	Definition	Max. Response Time (Seconds)
Key Print	Press key until appearance of character	0.2
XY EntEntry	Select field until visual verification	0.2
Point	Input of point to display of point	0.2
Sketch	Input to display of line	0.2
Local Update	Change using local data base	0.5
Page Turn	Request until first few lines visible	1.0
Function Selection	Selection until respose	2.0
Host Update	Change using readily accessible host date	2.0
Simple Inquiry	Display of commonly used message	2.0
Error Feedback	Entry of input until error message appears	2.0
File Update	Update requires access to host file	10.0
Complex Inquiry	Seldom used calculations in graphic form	10.0

Dialogue Design

6.43 Dialogue Considerations
Consider response time in choosing a dialogue.

When developing a human-computer interface for a system in which you have no control over the response time, take the system's response time characteristics into account when selecting the dialogue approach. Menu dialogues, for example, make quick responses critical to efficient user interaction. Immediate, directly observable results are also crucial elements of a direct manipulation dialogue. With a full-screen transaction dialogue, such as form-filling, short response times are also desirable, but moderate response times are less disruptive for form-filling dialogues than for menus and direct manipulation. *Martin, 1973*

6.44 Echo Delay
Echo user entries instantaneously.

Response time for echoing user entries, such as the time between pressing a character key on the keyboard and showing that character on the display, should appear to the user to be instantaneous. This requires delays of no more than 0.1 to 0.2 seconds. In point-to-select dialogues, the highlighting or marking of a selection is considered an echo, and should appear instantaneously. Auditory signals associated with selection should also occur instantaneously. *Gallaway, 1981; MIL-STD-1472C*

6.45 Interactive Delay
Respond to interactive requests in two seconds.

For an effective interactive dialogue, response time should be no more than 2 seconds, and preferably less.

IBM reports by Doherty and Kelisky (1979) and Thadhani (1981) have shown huge increases in the number of transactions programmers enter per unit time when response time is reduced to less than one second. They have characterized this as a productivity increase, but transaction volume is not necessarily a measure of usable work productivity. In fact, users tend to work faster and less carefully, make more errors, and generate more unproductive transactions when response time is especially fast, probably because the time cost of errors is less. *Gallaway, 1981; Shneiderman, 1980, 1983d*

6.46 File Delay
Load or save files within ten seconds.

Delays of up to 10 seconds may be acceptable for file access or updates, because these requests often come at major closure points in the user's action plan, and because users often expect and accept delays during file updates. Where practical, however, shorter response times are desirable. *MIL-STD-1472C, 1981*

Chapter Seven
Data Entry

This chapter presents techniques for requesting input from the user. This is perhaps the most critical aspect of the operator-computer interface. Poorly designed input procedures can make the system inaccessible to all but highly experienced users, while designs that simplify input can bring about effective interaction with little or no user training or experience. To minimize opportunities for typing errors, entries should be made by selecting from a list or entering a single character rather than by a typed command. Experienced users also require special attention in the design of input strategies. Unnecessarily cumbersome input requirements can impede and frustrate the skilled user who is impatient to proceed.

Errors by terminal users are inevitable. However, careful design of input procedures can reduce the frequency and consequences of errors and can simplify the correction of errors. A well-designed interactive system permits users to perform their jobs with a minimum of effort and time spent on keying entries. The following material presents means of simplifying the user's tasks in the input processes.

Prompts for Entries
7.1 Distinctive Prompts
Place prompts to be easily found.

Place input prompts so they are located easily and discriminated easily from other data on the same screen.

7.2 Location
Place prompts in standard locations.

Locate input prompts in consistent screen locations. *Granda, Teitelbaum, and Dunlap, 1982*

7.3 Cursor Positioning
Minimize cursor movement.

Arrange entry prompts to minimize requirements for cursor positioning. *Engel and Granda, 1975*

7.4 Automatic Cursor Positioning
The cursor starts at the first entry field.

When a form-filling display initially appears, the cursor is automatically placed at the first character position of the first entry field. *Galitz,1981*

7.5 Standardized Procedures
Use standardized input procedures.

Standardize procedures for data input. The format, location, grammatical structure, and input mode used for input prompts should be consistent throughout the system. *Galitz,1981*

7.6 Input Prompt Clarity
Use clear input prompts.

Make input prompts clear and understandable. They should not require reference to coding schemes or conventions that may be unfamiliar to occasional users.

USE

```
WEEK: _   MONTH: _ _   YEAR: _ _

SOCIAL SECURITY NO: _ _ _  _ _  _ _ _ _
```

DON'T USE

```
DATE CODE: _ _ _ _ _
SSN: _ _ _ _ _ _ _ _ _
```

7.7 Single Entry Prompts
Each input field has a prompt.

Each request or prompt applies to a single entry field.

USE

```
Last Name: _____
   Initials: __
Organization: ____
     Phone: ___ ____
```

DON'T USE

```
NAME, ORGANIZATION, AND PHONE NO.
```

7.8 Format Specifications
Show the correct input format.

Display the format required for an entry as part of the entry caption or prompt. *Galitz, 1981*

USE

```
STARTING DATE (DDMMYY): _____
```

DON'T USE

```
STARTING DATE:
```

7.9 Valid Options
Show valid options.

When the number of valid codes or options for an entry is small, display the valid options as part of the entry caption or prompt. Where space permits, also define each code.

USE

```
TRANSACTION CODE (A=ADD, C=CHANGE): _
```

DON'T USE

```
TRANSACTION CODE: _
```

7.10 Default Values
Show default values.

Where appropriate, display the currently defined default values for a data entry transaction. This can be accomplished:

1   by providing the default as part of the prompt or caption for an entry field, or

2   by pre-filling the entry field with the default, allowing the user to type over it if desired.

The second technique makes it important to identify the entry fields clearly (such as by preceding the input field with a prompt than ends in a colon). Because the entry field contains data initially, a standard input field indicator (the colon) is necessary to signal that the field is available for entry.

Example 1:

```
ERASE FILE?  (Y=YES, N or Blank=NO): _
```

Note:
In example 1, if the user enters either "N" or nothing, the system recognizes a "NO" answer. Only "Y" will cause the file to be erased.

Example 2:

```
HOURS WORKED THIS WEEK: 40
```

Note:
In example 2, the default value, 40, can be changed. The colon is used in the prompt to make it clear that, even though the number is generated by the computer, its value can be modified by typing over it.

Input Data Format
This section lists formatting guidelines to simplify the entry of data into type-in fields, such as in a form-filling dialogue. Appropriate design and placement of prompts, labels, and fill-in fields can have major benefits in reducing task time, errors, and training requirements.

7.11 Input Field Definition
Show the length of entry fields.

Use input prompts to indicate clearly how many input characters are required. Some methods for indicating field lengths are solid-line underscores, broken-line underscores, brackets, column separators, and reverse video. Solid-line underscores, brackets, and reverse video provide only an approximate visual indication of the number of input characters, so broken-line underscores or column separators are preferable. The best choice may depend on how each of the potential field length indicators is displayed on the specific display devices to be used. For example, if the cursor position indicator is identical to the underscore character, underscores should not be used as field length indicators. *Engel and Granda, 1975; Galitz,1981; Savage, Habinek, and Blackstad, 1982*

Examples:
In all these examples, the field length indicators are replaced by input characters as data are entered into the field.

Broken-line underscores
(preferred)   ACCOUNT NUMBER: _ _ _ _

Column separators
(preferred)   ACCOUNT NUMBER: | | | | | or
                  ACCOUNT NUMBER: . . .

Solid-line underscores
(not preferred) ACCOUNT NUMBER:_____

Brackets
(not preferred)   ACCOUNT NUMBER: <   >

Reverse video
(not preferred)   ACCOUNT NUMBER: [⬛⬛⬛⬛⬛]

No field indicators
(DON'T USE)   ACCOUNT NUMBER:

7.12 Finding the Cursor
Field length indicators do not obscure the cursor.

The choice of a field length indicator must take into consideration the kind of cursor(s) the system will use. An underscore cursor can be obscured by underscore field length indicators. A block cursor may be obscured by reverse video field indicators. A blinking cursor may help to overcome the "camouflage" of characters that are similar to the cursor symbol. *Savage, Habinek, and Blackstad, 1982*

7.13 Locating Labels
Locate caption to left of fields and above columns.

Place the label or caption for a single field to the left of the field. Locate the caption for a column of fields above the column. *Galitz, 1981; Engel and Granda, 1975*

Example:

```
┌─────────────────────────────────────────────────────┐
│  DIVISION: _ _ _ _      DEPARTMENT: _ _ _ _ _         │
│                                                        │
│  EMPLOYEE NAME        NUMBER   EXTENSION              │
│  _ _ _ _ _ _ _ _ _ _ _   _ _ _ _ _   _ _ _ _ _         │
│  _ _ _ _ _ _ _ _ _ _ _   _ _ _ _ _   _ _ _ _ _         │
│  _ _ _ _ _ _ _ _ _ _ _   _ _ _ _ _   _ _ _ _ _         │
│  _ _ _ _ _ _ _ _ _ _ _   _ _ _ _ _   _ _ _ _ _         │
└─────────────────────────────────────────────────────┘
```

127

7.14 Leading Zeros
Do not require leading zeros.

Leading zeros should be optional in entering data. For example, if a user enters the number 56 in a field that is four characters wide, the system should recognize it as 56 rather than requiring that 0056 or _ _ 56 be entered. It also must not interpret 56_ _ as 5600. *Engel and Granda, 1975; Galitz,1981*

ACCEPT

```
Units Sold:  5 6 _ _
```

DON'T REQUIRE

```
Units Sold:  0 0 5 6

       OR

Units Sold:  _ _ 5 6
```

7.15 Measurement Units
Display unit designators.

When a dimensional unit is used consistently with a particular entry field, the unit designator is displayed as part of a fixed label rather than entered by the user. When the dimensional unit varies for a given field, the user is permitted to enter the appropriate unit designator.

7.16 Familiar Units
Use familiar units.

Enter data in the units that are most familiar to the user. Necessary conversions should be made by the computer. *Patrick, 1980*

USE

```
Highway speed limit: _ _ _  miles per hour
```

DON'T USE

```
Highway speed limit: _ _ _  feet per second
```

Keyboard Entries
A well designed data entry dialogue can reduce the amount of time and effort required to get data into the computer. Many potential users are not skilled typists. Some hate to type or even refuse to type. Dialogues can be designed to reduce typing, require it only for free form text entry, or even eliminate the need for a keyboard in some applications.

7.17 Reduce Keying
Reduce keying requirements.

Design dialogs to reduce input requirements. Make input keywords short and have them approximate real words to reduce the amount of typing required. When possible, allow the user to select the item by entering its number or letter, or by pointing at its label or icon, rather than by requiring the entry of a longer item code or word.

Tradeoffs:

Reducing key strokes is generally desirable. However, in some situations, a technique that requires more key strokes may be preferable to one that is more confusing, more error-prone, or harder to remember. (For example, it is probably easier to press the cursor-down arrow four times than to remember and type "D4" for down four, even though D4 requires fewer key strokes.) *Engel and Granda, 1975*

7.18 Explicit Options
Make available options explicit.

Permit the user to select from a list of options, rather than requiring the memorizing and typing of commands. This reduces the number of key strokes as well as the amount of training required to operate the computer system effectively. *Elam, 1980*

7.19 Parameter Re-entry
Avoid requirements to re-enter data.

Do not require the user to re-enter parameters that have not changed since the previous interaction. *Engel and Granda, 1975*

Data Entry

7.20 System Data
Avoid type in data available to the system.

Avoid requiring the user to enter information already available to the system, such as the current date, terminal ID, and user number. *Smith and Aucella, 1983*

7.21 Truncated Commands
Allow truncation of commands.

Permit abbreviation of inputted commands. The system should recognize a command from the first one, two, or three letters (as necessary to make it distinct from other commands). Novice users can type in the entire command, while experienced users can abbreviate or truncate it. The system should accept either form. For example, if a P uniquely identifies a print command (no other commands start with P), it should be the user's option to enter either PRINT, PR, P, or any other truncation to initiate a print command. If the user enters too few letters for the computer to identify the command, the system should respond by listing the command options that fit the user's truncation and permit the user to select the intended command. *Ehrenreich, 1981*

7.22 Prompt Character
Prompts end with a colon.

Use a standard character, such as a colon, to denote a prompt for input; for example,

ENTER NAME: _
Galitz, 1981

7.23 Use of Colons
Use colons only for input prompts.

When colons are used to indicate input prompts, reserve them for that purpose only. This ensures that input prompts are uniquely identifiable. An exception to this restriction can be made to display time with hours, minutes, and seconds separated by colons, for example,
TIME =10:43:21 PM.

7.24 Optional Entries
Distinguish optional from required entries.

When some entries are optional and some are mandatory, the input prompts indicate which are optional. On color displays, optional and mandatory field length indicators can be shown in different colors.

USE

```
License number: _ _ _ _ _ _ _ _
      Make (optional): _ _ _ _ _ _ _ _ _ _ _ _ _ _
Year model (optional): _ _ _ _
```

7.25 Optional Entry Location
Mandatory inputs precede optional ones.

Locate entry fields so that the mandatory inputs are entered first, then the optional inputs. Thus, if users intend to enter only the mandatory inputs, they are not required to tab past interspersed optional inputs. Exceptions to this principle may be made when some other principle or ordering (such as compatibility with source data paper forms) takes precedence. *Galitz, 1981*

7.26 Complex Dependencies
Avoid complex entry dependencies.

Avoid complicated "If/Then" interdependency rules among input fields for valid entries. There is usually insufficient screen space to explain these rules adequately in instructions. Users will be confused when the screen's syntax is entry dependent. Errors, delays, and frustration are likely to result.

Example:
If "S" is entered in field 1, then fields 2 and 4 must be left blank; if "R" is entered in field 1, then field 2 must contain a number between 10 and 1000, and field 4 must be left blank; if "D" is entered in field 1, then field 3 must be left blank and fields 2 and 4 must both contain numbers between 10 and 1000. *Galitz, 1981*

7.27 Input Alteration
Inputs can be altered.

The user should be able to alter input during and after entry. For instance, a system should allow erasure or cursor repositioning for typing over previously entered input. The input specifications should remain on the screen when the requested data are displayed so that the user can easily alter portions of the input without having to re-enter all of it to generate a slightly different subset of the requested data. *Engel and Granda, 1975*

7.28 Command Prompt
Use a standard character to prompt for commands.

In a line-by-line interactive command language dialogue, provide a prompt symbol to indicate that a user command is requested. The term line-by-line dialogue is used here to mean a dialogue in which the user enters a command, typically a one-line entry, and the system responds, then waits for the next command (the typical teletype style of interaction).

USE (in a line-by-linedialogue)

```
ENTER
NAME
=> D. B. Bowman
ENTER DEPARTMENT
NUMBER => 129
```

DON'T USE

```
ENTER NAME
D. B. Bowman
ENTER DEPARTMENT
NUMBER 129
```

Note:
In this example the underlining signifies user entries and all characters that are not underlined are computer generated. *Engel and Granda, 1975*

Chapter Eight

Control and Display Devices

Traditionally, human-computer interfaces have relied heavily on the keyboard as the control device by which the user communicates with the computer. The recent popularity of direct manipulation and point-to-select dialogues have given new importance to cursor control and pointing devices such as the touch screen, mouse, joystick, trackball, and lightpen. This category of controls had previously been used mostly for either graphics input tasks, such as computer aided design, or tracking tasks, such as following or selecting the symbol for a target on the display screen.

Recent trends in user interface design, however, are reducing our reliance on keyboards and giving other control devices, such as cursor control and selection devices, a more central role in the user interface. In many newer applications the primary function of the keyboard is in the entry of free-form text data (for example, word processing) and numeric data. Many of the dialogue control functions are being allocated to other devices.

Unfortunately, scientific research into the optimal device for various categories of tasks, users, and environments has not been able to keep pace with the rapid growth in popularity of alternative control devices. The state of our knowledge is complicated by the problems of generalizing from the studies that have been conducted. Any study is typically conducted with subjects from a specialized user population, using a specific hardware and software environment, with specific response time characteristics, specific workplace and environmental characteristics, and a specific human-computer interface implementation approach. Until we have a solid base of many similar studies which give us a pattern of results under many combinations of the factors mentioned above, we usually cannot take the results of an isolated study and apply them in a different situation.

Fortunately, some guidelines can be offered for the selection of the appropriate control devices. Many of these relate to physical characteristics of the devices, such as arm support, resolution, and table space, rather than psychological factors contributing to ease of learning and ease of use. Considerable research momentum has developed in the psychological characteristics of various human-computer interface control devices, however, and more detailed guidance for the designer should be available soon.

Touch Sensitive Devices

Touch sensitive devices are display devices that permit the user to input a selection or designate a position on the display by touching the desired location or item with a finger or stylus. Four kinds of touch technologies are available:

1 Optical techniques detect the point at which the operator's finger or a pointer interrupts a grid of light or infrared beams over the surface of the display.

2 Acoustic techniques use ultrasonic waves, detecting the touch point by the timing of echoes reflected off the finger or pointer.

3 Capacitive techniques detect the capacitance introduced by the operator's finger at the touched location.

4 Resistance techniques use two transparent membranes embedded with a grid of electrodes. The pressure of a touch causes the electrodes in that location to make contact with each other, completing a circuit representing that location.

Table 8.1 summarizes the relative advantages and disadvantages of the four major touch technologies: optical, acoustic, capacitive, and resistance.

Table 8.1.   Comparison of Touch Device Technologies

Device	Resolution	Inadvertent Activation	Software Configurable	Touch With	Susceptible To
Optical	1/4"	Sensitive	Yes	Anything	Parallax
Acoustic	1/4"	Sensitive	Yes	Anything	Dirt,scratches
Capacitive	1/2"	No	No	Finger only	Temp.,humidity
Resistance	Pixel	Less likely	Yes	Anything	Misalignment

(Based on Tyler, 1983; Pfauth and Priest, 1981)

8.1 Touch Selection
Use touch devices for selecting.

Touch sensitive panels and touch screen CRT devices can provide effective software–driven analogues to electro-mechanical control devices such as push buttons. Users can benefit if the devices are programmed to simulate familiar physical controls. Menu selections, for example, can simulate physical push buttons.

Touch devices allow greater flexibility than electro-mechanical controls by providing the capability to reconfigure the number, location, size, shape, and labels of the touch sensitive fields under software control. In contrast to mechanical controls, options can be displayed only when needed, rather than having to be present continually. *Nakatani and Rohrlich, 1983; Pfauth and Priest, 1981*

8.2 Touch Devices
Use touch devices for intermittent inputs.

Touch device implementations often require users to hold the full weight of their arms without the benefit of supporting surfaces. If an installation does not permit a mounting scheme which provides arm support during touch device usage, the role of the touch device should be restricted to short duration, intermittent functions. Prolonged, intensive touch device usage may cause undue muscle strain, impaired performance, and errors. *Pfauth and Priest, 1981*

8.3 Arm Support
Provide arm support for touch device users.

If a touch sensitive panel or touch screen is to be used for functions which require continuous interaction, its mounting should provide for support of the user's arm.

8.4 Accidental Touch Activation
Design to minimize accidental activation.

Some touch device technologies are susceptible to accidental activation. An optical sensor (infrared) touch device, for example, may be activated by a dropped pencil or sheet of paper. The human–computer interface design can compensate for this by requiring two steps to activate any critical, irreversible, or potentially damaging action. First the user touches the desired action, then touches an "ENTER" or "EXECUTE" function to initiate the selected action. This greatly reduces the probability of an accidental activation. Touch accuracy can also be enhanced by an ENTER function, although speed of input will suffer to some extent. *Albert, 1982*

8.5 Touch Device Resolution
Use touch for coarse positioning.

Touch screen and touch panel devices are effective for approximate positioning tasks, such as simulated push buttons for menu selection, but not for tasks requiring precise positioning tolerances, such as graphical input, drawing, and computer–aided design. Some touch technologies have resolution as coarse as 1/2 inch or more. (See Table 8.1.) Others have resolution to the pixel in theory, but the size of the user's finger and the parallax potential of the screen limit the effective resolution to 1/4 inch at best. The obstruction of the user's view of the display by the hand results in additional interference in precise positioning. *Albert, 1982; Beringer and Peterson, 1983; Pfauth and Priest, 1981; Tyler, 1983*

8.6 Touch Button Size
Use large touch sensitive areas.

Use large touch sensitive areas or soft buttons to reduce errors that activate the wrong button. MIL-STD-1472C recommends a minimal soft button size of 3/4 inch high by 3/4 inch wide plus at least 1/8 inch separation between touch sensitive areas. *Beringer and Peterson, 1985*

8.7 Touch Feedback
Provide touch selection feedback.

Provide auditory and visual feedback when the user touches a soft button. Without the tactile feedback provided by pressing a "hard" key, other forms of feedback are especially important. An auditory tone or beep signals the user that an input has been accepted. Visual feedback, such as displaying the activated touch area in reverse video or displaying a thick box outline around it, permits the user to verify that the intended button was activated. *Beringer and Peterson, 1985*

Control and Display Devices

Mouse

A mouse is a small cursor control device about the size of a deck of cards. It has rollers or optical sensors underneath which transduce the movements of the mouse on the table top to electrical signals. These signals direct the movement of the cursor on the screen in accordance with the movement of the mouse on the table top. The mouse may also have one or more buttons on top that may be used to select or act upon the item on the screen at which the cursor points.

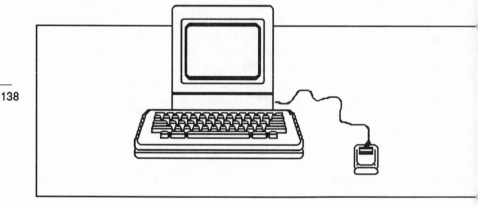

Figure 8.1
Example of a Mouse

8.8 Mouse Cursor Control
Use mouse for cursor-intensive tasks.

The mouse is well adapted to tasks which require frequent and moderately precise cursor positioning. It provides quick cursor movement across long screen distances (in contrast to cursor control arrow keys). A mouse provides accurate fine resolution cursor positioning. It also allows the table top to support the weight of the user's arm during prolonged usage, thus minimizing muscular fatigue (in contrast to touch devices or light pens). Some experimental studies (Card, English, and Burr, 1978; Reinhart and Marken, 1985) and technology writers (Lu, 1984) have recommended the mouse as the most satisfactory general purpose pointing device.

8.9 Mouse Uses
Use a mouse for selecting and dragging.

The mouse is useful for functions which require pointing, cursor selection, coarse drawing, and "dragging" graphical images or objects around on the screen. Its integration of selection button(s) with cursor movements gives it more flexibility than a simple cursor control. For example, the mouse can be used to point the cursor at an item on the screen, then the button can be pressed to "grasp" the item and "hold" it while the mouse is moved to drag it across the screen. When the item has been moved to the desired location, the button can be released to "drop" the item. This capability makes the mouse quite compatible with visual interfaces and graphical manipulation. *Shneiderman, 1982b*

8.10 Mouse–Keyboard Switching
Avoid frequent mouse-keyboard switches.

Avoid requiring users to make frequent changes from keyboard to mouse. In keyboard–intensive tasks, such as word processing, provide the necessary functions on the keyboard (for example, cursor control keys) to permit the user to perform the task from the keyboard. Frequent changes from keyboard to mouse and back interfere with the flow, and thus the efficiency, of keyboard tasks. The users must reorient their hands to the keyboard after each mouse use.

8.11 *Mouse Disadvantages*
Extra table space is required.

The mouse requires extra table or desk space on which it can be moved for cursor positioning. At least one square foot of flat, horizontal space must be left clear. This reduces the amount of space in the perimeter of the terminal that can be used for documents or additional equipment. In some situations, the trailing cord on the mouse may also present console layout or maintenance problems. For example, in mobile, airborne, or shipboard applications, devices that can be affixed to the console may be preferable to a mouse.

8.12 *Mouse Alternative*
Use mouse for many targets, jump keys for few targets.

The mouse is an effective pointing and selecting device when there is a potential for a large number of targets from which to select by pointing. However, when the dialogue never requires more than six to eight targets, left- and right-arrow jump keys may be preferable. Jump keys are like tab keys that cause the cursor to move to the next selectable target, either to the left and above (left-arrow key), or to the right and below (right-arrow key). They permit the user's hands to remain on the keyboard during pointing, thus eliminating mouse-keyboard switching. Jump keys become cumbersome, however, as the number of potential targets increases.

Fixed Function Keys
A fixed function key is a keyboard button with a predefined, unchanging function. The name or symbol for that function is typically engraved or printed onto the key cap.

| PRINT | HELP | SAVE | ESCAPE | UNDO |

Figure 8.2.
Fixed Function Keys

8.13 Common Functions
Use fixed function keys for common functions.

Fixed function keys are used for universal functions that are likely to be used in a wide variety of applications. Proper selection and use of fixed functions can provide a mechanism for diverse applications to perform common functions in the same way. This can simplify learning of new applications and reduce the likelihood of negative transfer, which can occur when different programs require different user responses to initiate the same function.

Examples of functions that may be candidates for fixed function key implementation include PAGE FORWARD, PAGE BACK, PRINT, HELP, SAVE (but always require confirmation before over-writing existing files), ESCAPE, CANCEL, UNDO, and various field tabbing and cursor control keys. Those selected should be common to a wide variety of the applications that the system will run, and the applications should be designed to use the fixed functions in identical or analogous ways.

8.14 Fixed Function Use
Use fixed keys for frequent, critical functions.

Reserve fixed function keys for important functions, such as those that are used very frequently or those that are critical to effective or safe performance of tasks.

8.15 Active Functions
Show which functions are active.

When some fixed functions are only available in certain situations or at certain stages of the dialogue, it is desirable to show which keys are currently active if the equipment provides the capability. Examples include backlighted keys or small lights such as LEDs imbedded in the keys. Only those functions that are currently active are lit. *Hollingsworth and Dray, 1981; Smith and Mosier, 1984*

Program Function Keys
Program function keys are multi–purpose keys that can be used for different functions in different programs or at different places in the same program. They are typically engraved with key numbers such as F1, F2, F3, or PF1, PF2, PF3, and so on.

Control and Display Devices

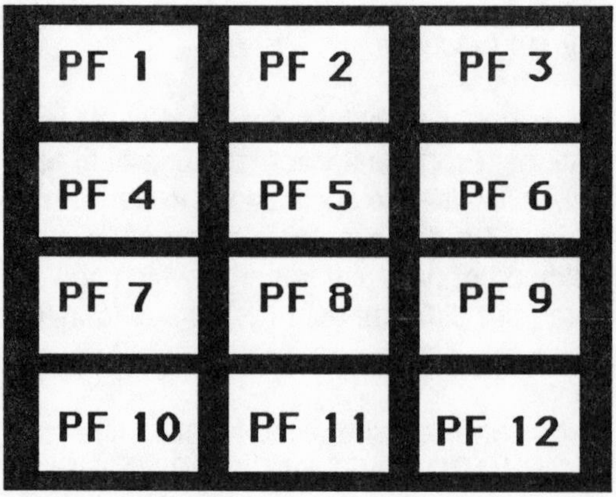

PF 1	PF 2	PF 3
PF 4	PF 5	PF 6
PF 7	PF 8	PF 9
PF 10	PF 11	PF 12

Figure 8.3
Program Function Keys

8.16 Dedicated Functions
Use dedicated functions for critical or frequent inputs.

User-terminal interaction tasks that are repetitive, time-consuming, or complex can be simplified by assigning dedicated functions (usually single user actions) in system design. These actions should be accomplished by labeled fixed function keys, dedicated program function keys, dedicated light pen, mouse or touch fields.

Functions are assigned to dedicated function keys based on the following criteria. Dedicated functions are used for

1 time-critical,

2 error-critical, or

3 frequently used control inputs.

Do not dedicate function keys to trivial, seldom used functions.
Elam, 1980; MIL-STD-1472C, 1981.

8.17 Function Key Display.
Identify function keys.

Display pertinent program function key assignments at all times. The assigned key functions for the variable functions are displayed on each screen. If some standard functions are sometimes inactive, the displayed assignments should either show only currently active functions or label the temporarily unavailable functions with an "inactive" indicator. *Brown et al, 1980,1983; Smith and Mosier, 1984*

8.18 Consistent Functions
Assign program functions keys consistently.

Once a function has been assigned to a given variable function key, do not reassign it later to a different key. Throughout the system, however, the same key may have to be assigned to different functions as required by the tasks to be performed.

Examples:
Do not use F1=RESTART on one transaction and F2=RESTART on another. It is acceptable, however, to use F1=RESTART in one place and F1=CLEAR INPUT in another.

8.19 Function Key Location
Consider key layout in assigning function keys.

When assigning functions to a given set of program function keys, consider the geometry of the keypad and the spatial relations among the functions. In a single row of keys, the end keys, especially the leftmost key, are most accessible. In a matrix of keys, the corner keys (especially the top left key) are more accessible than interior keys. Also, spatial relationships among the functions can often be reflected in the geometrical relationship of the keys.

Examples:

1   The HELP program function key should often be the most accessible function. Assign it to the upper left key.
2   TAB LEFT should be located beside and to the left of TAB RIGHT.
3   PAGE BACK should be located beside and to the left of PAGE AHEAD.

Example of a Row of Program Function Keys

F1 F2 F3 F4 F5 F6 F7 F8 F9 F10
|| ||
Most Accessible   Accessible

Example of a Matrix of Program Function Keys

Most Accessible-->	F1	F2	F3 <--Accessible
	F4	F4	F6
	F7	F8	F9
Accessible-->	F10	F11	F12 <--Accessible

Figure 8.4. Accessible Program Function Keys

Light Pen

A light pen is a stylus connected by a cord to the terminal which provides a signal permitting the terminal to detect the screen location where the light pen is pressed.

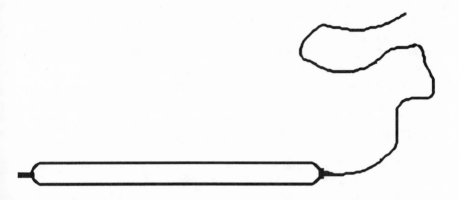

Figure 8.5.
Light Pen

8.20 Light Pen
Use light pens to select, move cursor, and draw.

Light pens are useful devices for selecting from menus by pointing the stylus at the desired option(s). They may also be used for cursor positioning and for graphical input tasks such as drawing or computer aided design.

8.21 Prolonged Light Pen Use
Avoid prolonged light pen use.

Light pen implementations seldom provide any support to user's arms. This makes the light pen undesirable for tasks which would require intensive, continual use of the light pen without frequent opportunities to rest the arm. *Ramsey and Atwood, 1979*

8.22 Light Pen Switching
Avoid alternation from light pen to keyboard.

Computer dialogues must not require users to alternate between light pen and keyboard entry unnecessarily. When dialogs that require keyboard entry at some stages permit menu selection by light pen at other stages, use of the light pen should be optional. Users are permitted to make selections from the keyboard if they desire. Thus, users are not required to take their hands away from the keyboard, pick up and use the light pen, then put down the light pen and orient themselves on the keyboard. *Engel and Granda, 1975*

8.23 Light Pen Fields
Make light pen selectable fields large.

The fields defined as light pen selectable (the poke points) are as large as possible. As a minimum, make all of the text associated with an option selectable, not just the option number. The light pen is not accurate as a placement device because of parallax problems and screen curvature. Larger fields help to reduce these problems. In the following example, the underscores indicate light pen selectable fields or poke points.

USE

```
SELECT NEXT ACTION WITH LIGHT PEN.
  1.  REWIND FILE
  2.  DELETE FILE
  3.  READ NEXT FILE
```

DON'T USE

```
SELECT NEXT ACTION WITH LIGHT PEN
  1. REWIND FILE
  2. DELETE FILE
  3. READ NEXT FILE
```

Engel and Granda, 1975; Smith and Aucella, 1983

Voice Entry

Voice data entry devices have become a viable option for certain kinds of human–computer interface functions. Isolated word voice entry systems recognize units of speech called utterances, which may correspond to a word or phrase. With most current speech recognition devices the speaker must pause after each utterance so the recognition device can identify the end of the unit of vocal input. The device then compares the utterance with templates of sound patterns stored in its data base. *Simpson, McCauley, Roland, Ruth, and Williges, 1985*

The data base is typically created by having each user repeat the phrases that will be equated to system commands later, and the machine forms templates to match the sound patterns of each utterance. Although some degree of recognition is possible with a generic set of templates, it is usually necessary to train the machine separately for the voice of each user to achieve satisfactory recognition accuracy. When a given person is using the system, only the templates developed on that person's voice are used for matching. *Michaelis, 1984*

Many systems provide a display device or voice synthesizer to echo each command, as interpreted by the voice recognizer, back to the user. The user then has the opportunity to correct the entry before it is executed. The user may say, for example, "Wrong" when a misrecognized utterance is echoed and "Correct" when recognition is correct.

The guidelines that follow in this section assume currently available voice data entry technology. Efforts are underway to develop computer systems with the capability to accept natural, continuous speech rather than separated, discrete utterances. Artificial intelligence research is also being applied in attempts to permit computers to utilize natural language in communicating with users (Rich, 1984). When these new technologies become mature, many of the limitations of voice entry that are mentioned here may no longer apply.

8.24 Voice Command Entry
Use voice to enter commands and numbers.

Voice data entry is well suited for inputting discrete, simple commands and numbers, particularly low volume inputs when speed is not critical. Voice entry of a large volume of numbers, as in a keypunch task, would be too slow to be practical in most situations.

8.25 Voice and Workload
Use voice when hands or eyes are not free.

Perhaps the most useful application of current voice data entry
technology is in jobs which require the operator to use his hands or eyes
for tasks other than data entry. Voice entry can also be used when
operator mobility is required or in a hostile environment, such as
underwater.

Example:
In an inspection task the operator must manipulate and visually examine
the inspected item. If the operator is required to type the part number and
the inspection results into a keyboard, that will slow his inspection rate
down considerably. If, however, the inspector can speak the part number
and inspection data into a voice entry device, the inspection and the
entry of data can occur simultaneously.

8.26 Voice Device Training
Voice entry is best for predesignated users.

Voice entry is most appropriate for applications in which all those who will
use the system can be identified in advance of use and the voice entry
device can be trained to each user's voice. Voice entry may not be
effective when some users are not able to pre–train the device.

Current voice entry devices require templates of each user's voice to
achieve high voice–recognition accuracy. Each user must train the
device to his or her specific vocal patterns by repeating many times each
utterance that will subsequently be used as a command. Later, when
starting to operate the system, the user first identifies himself. The
system then retrieves a user–specific set of vocal templates and
compares user utterances against these.

8.27 Voice and Stress
Avoid voice entry in stressful applications.

Stress causes changes in the sound patterns of the human voice that
result in degraded recognition of utterances by voice entry devices.
Voice entry should thus be avoided for stressful tasks, or tasks that could
potentially require emergency responses. *Simpson et al., 1985*

8.28 Voice and Noise
Avoid voice entry in noisy environments.

Noisy environments can reduce voice recognition accuracy, both by introducing extraneous sound into the recognition device and by causing the user to speak differently than he or she would in quiet. Voice entry should thus be used only in low to moderate noise environments (less than 85 dB SPL). *Simpson et al., 1985*

Joystick
A joystick is a lever with one end mounted in a transducer device. The angular movement of the joystick is translated to electrical signals, which cause the cursor to move in a direction corresponding to the movement of the joystick. A force stick or stiff stick is a variant in which the stick does not move, but cursor movements are controlled by the amount and direction of force applied to the stick.

149

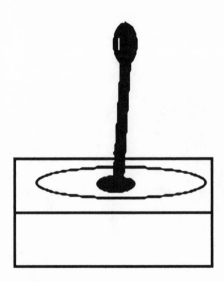

Figure 8.6
Joystick

8.29 Joystick Uses
Use joystick to move cursor and to track.

The joystick is an effective cursor positioning device. It permits precise positioning as well as quick movement over large screen distances. Joysticks are also well suited to tracking tasks, which require the user to follow a moving element on the screen with the cursor. A joystick can be built into the keyboard to permit easier integration of cursor positioning and keyboard usage.

Trackball
A trackball is a ball about two to five inches in diameter that can be rotated within a fixed housing. The user turns the exposed part of the ball with the palm or fingers. The rotation of the ball is transduced to electrical signals which direct the motion of the cursor on the screen.

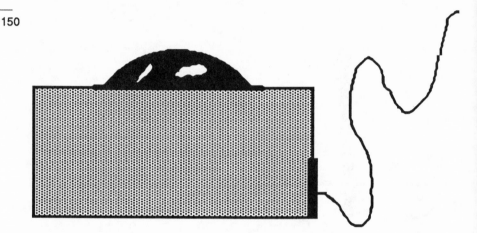

Figure 8.7
Trackball

8.30 Trackball Uses
Use trackball to move cursor and to track.

A trackball is an effective device for fine cursor control and for cursor movements over long screen distances. It can be integrated into or next to the keyboard to minimize the interference of cursor positioning on keyboard–intensive tasks. Trackballs are also effective for tracking tasks.

8.31 Handedness
Cursor device design considers handedness.

Cursor control device design should permit easy use for both right and left handed users. Fine cursor control tasks will usually require use of the preferred hand. Cursor control devices such as joysticks and trackballs should thus be mounted either in a separate module from the keyboard that can be placed on either side of the keyboard, or with two controls, one on each side of the keyboard.

Keyboard
The alphanumeric keyboard is the most commonly used computer input device. Many guidelines related to its use are presented in Chapter Seven: Data Entry. Most of the guidelines listed here deal with the physical aspects of keyboard use in human-computer interface design.

8.32 Alphanumeric Keyboard
Use alphanumeric keyboard as general purpose entry device.

The alphanumeric keyboard is a versatile device that is useful for entering text, numbers, commands, and selections.

8.33 Cursor Control Keys
Use cursor keys for short cursor movements.

Cursor control keys are useful for short, discrete movements of the cursor to character positions. Cursor movements over long screen distances using cursor control keys are slow. Cursor control keys are usually not effective for tasks which require precise cursor positioning, such as graphical input or manipulation tasks. The mouse, joystick, and trackball are better for these tasks.

8.34 Compatible Cursor Keys
Key layout is compatible with movement.

The arrangement of the cursor control keys on the keyboard should be compatible with the direction of cursor movement each key generates. An example of a compatible layout is shown in Figure 8.7.

8.35 Repeating Keys
Cursor keys repeat when held down.

Cursor movement should continue as long as the cursor control key is held down. This permits longer movements without repeated key presses.

8.36 Faster Cursor Keys
Provide double speed cursor mode.

152   A useful keyboard feature provides a key which, when pressed in conjunction with the normal cursor control keys, causes the cursor to move two positions at a time as long as the double speed key is pressed. When the cursor approaches the vicinity of the target location, the double speed key can be released (with the cursor key still pressed) and the cursor will move one space at a time. The key labelled "Fast" in Figure 8.7 is an example.

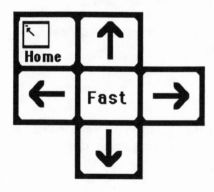

Figure 8.8.
Cursor Control Key Layout

8.37 Jump Keys
Arrow keys can be used as jump keys.

Arrow keys (tab keys or cursor keys) can be used to expedite cursor selection if they are programmed to cause the cursor to jump to the next (right-arrow) or previous (left-arrow) selectable target. *Shneiderman, 1985*

8.38 Numeric Keypad
Use numeric key pads for massed entry of numbers.

Numeric keypads can permit faster entry of data that consists exclusively of numbers than is possible using the numeric keys on the typewriter–style alphanumeric keyboard.

Summary
Table 8.2 summarizes the uses, advantages, and disadvantages of various control devices. It is based in part on *Card, Burr, and English, 1978; Olsen, 1981; Williams and Olsen ,1980*

8.37 Jump Keys
Arrow keys can be used as jump keys.

Arrow keys (tab keys or cursor keys) can be used to expedite cursor selection if they are programmed to cause the cursor to jump to the next (right-arrow) or previous (left-arrow) selectable target. *Shneiderman, 1985*

8.38 Numeric Keypad
Use numeric key pads for massed entry of numbers.

Numeric keypads can permit faster entry of data that consists exclusively of numbers than is possible using the numeric keys on the typewriter–style alphanumeric keyboard.

Summary
Table 8.2 summarizes the uses, advantages, and disadvantages of various control devices. It is based in part on *Card, Burr, and English, 1978; Olsen, 1981; Williams and Olsen ,1980*

Table 8.2 Control Devices

Device	Uses	Disadvantages
Touch Sensitive Panel or Touch Screen CRT	Select	Accidental activation; Tires arms
Mouse	Point; Select; Draw Drag; Move cursor	Requires desk space; Has trailing cord
Fixed Function Keys	Frequent or critical functions	Keyboard space permits limited number of keys
Program Function Keys	Application-specific functions	Meanings change; No direct labelling
Light Pen	Move cursor; Select; Draw	Parallax; Tires arm
Voice Entry	Enter numbers; Initiate predefined actions	Requires step-by-step confirmation of entries
Joystick	Track; Select; Move cursor	Mouse may be faster for selecting text
Trackball	Track; Select; Move cursor	Mouse may be faster for selecting text
Alphanumeric Keyboard	Select; Enter text; enter numbers	Suboptimal for graphics and direct manipulation
Cursor Control Keys	Discrete cursor movement	Slow for moving cursor long distances
Numeric Keypad	Enter numbers (keypunch)	Limited value for other tasks

Table 8.2 Control Devices (continued)

Recommended For	Not Recommended	Comments
Infrequent use; Coarse pointing	Continuous use; Precise pointing	Mount to provide arm rest
Tasks requiring little keyboard use	Frequent mouse to keyboard changes	Can integrate function buttons with cursor
Continuously available, important functions	Seldom used, noncritical functions	Label keys with function names
Frequently used or critical functions	Seldom used, noncritical functions	Define keys on display screen
Infrequent use; Tasks with little keyboard use	Frequent pen-keyboard changes;Continuous use	Mount display to provide armrest
When hands or eyes are not free	Noisy or stressful environments	Recognition of fluent speech not practical
Tasks with intensive cursor positioning	Frequent changes to and from keyboard	Provide for left-handed users
Integrating graphics with keyboard entries	Frequent changes to and from keyboard	Provide for left-handed users
General purpose entry device	Selection by typing slower than by pointing	Use standard layout for typewriter keys
Tasks requiring short cursor movements	Extensive or fine cursor movements	Provide "double speed"mode
Fast entry of massed numbers; Calculations	Infrequent numbers; Mixed text & numbers	Provide for left-handed users

Chapter Nine

Error Messages and Online Assistance

Error handling is a critical feature of effective human-computer interface design. Three main elements of error handling are error correction, error messages, and online guidance to help users understand the system and thus avoid errors.

■ Error Correction

The error correction guidelines presented below address the way in which the computer system detects errors, indicates their occurrence to users, and permits the user to correct them.

9.1 Program Response
Provide a response to every input.

The computer system responds to all user inputs, whether valid or invalid. For an invalid input, the system displays a message that indicates the entry is invalid and guides the user toward a valid one. For valid input, the computer displays the requested data or, if the requested transaction does not require a change in the displayed data, the computer presents a message acknowledging that the request has been accepted.

9.2 Error Recovery
Input remains after error.

Previously entered data are not lost after an error has been detected. The input data remain on the screen after the error message has been displayed to permit type-over correction of erroneous fields without requiring re-entry of correct data. *Elam, 1980; Engel and Granda, 1975; Shneiderman, 1979*

9.3 Multistep Transaction Errors
Allow correction at the point of first error.

When an error occurs in a transaction with multiple steps, permit users to correct the erroneous data and continue from the point the error was made. Do not require them to start the whole transaction over from step one. *Jones, 1978*

Example:
In the example below, computer prompts are designated by all capital letters and user entries or selections are designated by lower case letters.

USE

```
MONEY TREE INSTANT BANKER
INSERT CARD
ENTER ID NUMBER:1234
SELECT ACTION: withdrawal
SELECT ACCOUNT: checking
ENTER AMOUNT: $50
AMOUNT MUST BE
 MULTIPLE OF $20
RE-ENTER AMOUNT: $40
(The machine delivers $40 cash)
```

DON'T USE

```
MONEY TREE INSTANT BANKER
INSERT CARD
ENTER ID NUMBER:1234
SELECT ACTION: withdrawal
SELECT ACCOUNT: checking
ENTER AMOUNT: $50
AMOUNT MUST BE  MULTIPLE
OF  $20
(The machine ejects the bank card)
MONEY TREE INSTANT BANKER
INSERT CARD
(The user must start over.)
```

9.4 Error Message Display
Display error messages on entry screen.

Show error messages on the same screen format display as the erroneous input. This permits the user to refer to the original input while interpreting the error message, and then to make appropriate corrections. Do not require the user to page to a special error message display screen to view the message and then to page back to the input screen to correct the error.

Exception:
Exceptions may be necessary when massed data are submitted for editing, processing, or storage. For example, the data may have been accumulated without editing by a separate system. In these "store and forward" situations, it may be better to present error messages on a separate screen or printout, especially if a large number of messages is anticipated.

9.5 Highlight Errors
Highlight fields in error.

Highlight all data fields that have been edited and found to contain errors. This practice will aid users in finding and correcting errors. Simultaneously highlighting all fields in error also permits the user to correct several errors with a single transaction.

Error Messages and Online Assistance

9.6 Missing Entries

Show fields requiring missing data.

When an error due to failure to enter data in a mandatory field is detected, identify the fields in which an entry is required. Displaying a highlighted question mark (?) in each field for which an entry is missing is one effective technique.

9.7 Cursor Positioning

Position cursor at first error.

After an error is detected, automatically position the cursor at the first character of the entry field that contains the first error.

9.8 Old Messages

Remove error messages after correction.

Do not permit error messages to remain on the screen after the error has been corrected. *Peterson, 1979*

9.9 Auditory Error Signals

Use auditory signals conservatively.

If auditory signals (such as bells or beeps) are used to alert the user to an error, restrict the use of the signals for other purposes. Over use of auditory signals can defeat their purpose and may also annoy users or embarrass them if the signals are associated with errors. Consider providing a mechanism for the user to turn non-critical auditory signals off or to control their volume.

USE

An auditory beep signals that an error has been detected and that an explanatory message is being displayed in the standard error message location. This will help ensure that the user notices that a message has been displayed.

DON'T USE

Auditory beeps used for error detection, end-of-message signals, and as prompts when user entries are displayed. If the beeps are used for too many purposes, the user may tend to ignore them.

Error Messages

Error messages are intended to guide new, inexperienced, and occasionally, expert users in the efficient use of a system. Clear, concise, courteous, and meaningful error messages will increase user acceptance and efficiency in learning and using the system. *Galitz, 1980*

9.10 Useful Error Messages
Make error messages instructive.

Error messages should always state (or clearly imply) at least:

1 what error has been detected,
2 which input field contains the error, or
3 what corrective action to take.
  Engel and Granda, 1975; Pew and Rollins, 1975; Shneiderman 1979

USE

Part number format must be two letters, then three digits.

DON'T USE

Invalid input.

9.11 Polite Phrasing
Make error messages polite.

Error messages should be phrased politely. They should not place fault, use patronizing language, or attempt to be humorous.
Engel and Granda, 1975; Galitz, 1980, 1981; Peterson, 1979; Pew and Rollins, 1975

USE

The part number must be numbers only. Please reenter.

DON'T USE

You idiot! That part number has letters in it! Can't you do anything right?

9.12 Brief Messages
Make error messages brief.

Error messages should be brief but informative. Explanatory information can be presented in greater detail in the system documentation or through online HELP messages. *Galitz, 1981*

USE

> The MEMBER NUMBER must be a 3-digit number.

DON'T USE

> Alphabetic entries are not acceptable here
> because this entry will be processed arithmetically.
> Entry must be numeric.

162

9.13 Message Content
Make error messages appropriate to users.

The content of error messages should be appropriate to the user's level of knowledge. Error messages that may be useful to system analysts often are of little or no value to system users. *Shneiderman, 1982a*

USE

> The contract number you entered is not in the file.
> Please enter an active number.

DON'T USE

> R2805 PRS ASSY - SLD6961844 GET HOLD UNIQUE FAILED.

9.14 Consistent Messages
Use consistent error messages.

Use the same error message each time the same error occurs.

9.15   Specific Messages
Make error messages specific.

Do not use the same generic error message for a broad class of related but distinctly different errors. *Elam, 1980*

USE

> The TIME PERIOD must be W (week), M (month), or Y (year).

DON'T USE

> INVALID INPUT

9.16   Directive Messages
Use directive error messages.

Word error messages to direct users to correct the error. Appropriate use of the words must be or must have in error messages tends to produce clear, diagnostic messages. Use the following format:

> X MUST BE Y   or   X MUST HAVE Y

where X is the name of the field in error and Y is one of the following: the action required to correct the error, the correct format for the field, or a list of valid entries for the field.

USE

> The HOURS/DOLLARS CODE must be H for Hours or D for Dollars.

DON'T USE

> INVALID HOURS/DOLLARS CODE

9.17 Show Ranges
Show valid ranges and values in error messages.

Include the permissible values or ranges of values for the field in error in the error message.

USE

| The YEAR must be 1975 to 1995. |

DON'T USE

| ILLEGAL YEAR |

9.18 Affirmative Messages
Make error messages affirmative.

Error messages are usually more easily interpreted as affirmative statements than as negative statements. Negative messages often permit more than one interpretation and sometimes even permit contradictory interpretations. For example, the message PART CODE NOT NUMERIC could be interpreted as either "The part code you entered was not numeric, but is should have been numeric", or, "The part code is not a numeric field, but you tried to enter numeric data".

USE

| The PART CODE must be 3 digits. |

DON'T USE

| PART CODE NOT NUMERIC. |

Exception:
For the category of errors for which data do not exist, cannot be found, or cannot be retrieved, clear and unambiguous negative error messages, such as, "The data you requested are not on file", can be used. *Galitz, 1981*

9.19 Positive Tone
Avoid harsh, condemning words in messages.

Use words with a positive tone of constructive advice in error messages. Avoid words that imply blame, failure, or tragic consequences. Examples of words to be avoided include INVALID, ILLEGAL, and FATAL. Often the best way to rewrite a harsh message is to state the procedure for correction, rather than focusing on the error itself. *Shneiderman, 1982a*

USE

> The options for TIME PERIOD are D (day), W (week), and Y (year).

DON'T USE

> ERROR: ILLEGAL TIME PERIOD

9.20 Error Help Function
Provide levels of help.

Users should be able to control the amount of detail they receive in the explanation of errors. The HELP function can be used to present additional information when requested by a user. Successive HELP requests or continuation pages can go into greater detail, ultimately referring the user to documentation. *Shneiderman ,1979.*

9.21 System Abort
Keep user errors from aborting a session.

No user error should cause a session to be terminated or aborted.

9.22 System Protection
Keep user errors from destroying data.

Protection should be provided against costly user errors. One or more verification inputs should be required of the user to implement any action from which recovery is difficult or impossible, such as erasing a file. For example:

> Enter next action: D
> If deleted, this file will no longer be retrievable.
> Delete File (Y/N): Y

Engel and Granda, 1975

9.23 Message Data Base
Separate message text from programs.

Create a file, table, or data base to contain the error message text. Programs need only contain a message number to access the text from this file. The messages can then be reviewed and revised when problems are discovered in the original wording. Changes in wording can be made by non-programmers without requiring alteration of the applications programs.

9.24 Error Records
Provide for recording of user errors.

The system monitors and records user errors, either continuously or on a sampling basis. This information will be helpful in the design of future systems and in improving current systems. *Elam 1980; Shneiderman, 1982a*

9.25 Error Documentation
Document user messages.

List and explain all error messages in the system documentation and in an online HELP function.

Online Guidance
Much of the information commonly provided in paper documentation, such as user manuals, should also be available online. A manual may not be available when it is needed. Some users may never receive the relevant documentation. They may not know what documents are available, which ones are relevant, or how to procure them. Even users who have the appropriate paper documentation will not necessarily have it with them when they need it.

Paper documentation also tends to quickly become obsolete. Producing, updating, and distributing manuals is unwieldy and expensive. Online documentation can thus not only provide the user with more timely, accurate, and accessible guidance, but can also be much cheaper to develop and maintain than paper manuals. *Brown et al, 1980,1983; Limanowski, 1983*

9.26 Online Assistance
Provide online reference material.

Provide extensive online user assistance. An easily accessible reference system can serve several important purposes. It can be a valuable source of information to aid in recovery from errors. It can serve as a dictionary of codes and terminology. A summary of system capabilities and structure can be presented. Training requirements can be reduced by providing online instruction and guidance.

9.27 Online Access
Provide online system information .

Provide online access to a list of system capabilities and subsystems. Many systems are underutilized by experienced users as well as by novices because the full range of capabilities is not recognized. By showing the system components, options, and structure, the online reference capability permits the user to understand the system and use it more effectively. This capability may be implemented in the HELP procedure.

9.28 HELP Function
Provide a HELP function.

Online access to HELP facilities is provided for each screen. A HELP function might be designed to be used in the following manner: The user can request HELP from any screen in the interaction sequence. The system responds by displaying a HELP screen or window that presents the commands or messages most likely to require explanation. If more details are needed, the user can ask for continuation pages; if not, the user can return directly to the point from which the HELP function was called. *Galitz, 1980*

9.29 HELP Contents
HELP explains screens, fields, codes and messages.

The categories of assistance that may be useful in HELP displays include the following:

1   a brief explanation of the purpose of the screen or transaction,

2   descriptions of input fields (definitions, units, formats, valid entries),

3   descriptions of output data fields (definitions, units, formats, how values are calculated),

4   definition of codes, commands, and abbreviations used,

Error Messages and Online Assistance

5 error message explanations and error recovery hints,

6 program function key assignments, and

7 examples of correct procedures, commands, or syntax. *Brown, 1982; Limanowski, 1983*

9.30 List of Abbreviations
Provide list of abbreviations.

Provide an alphabetical list of abbreviations with their definitions online. This glossary can be incorporated into the HELP facility. *Brown et al, 1980,1983*

9.31 List of Commands
Provide an online command glossary.

168   For systems that use commands, provide an online list of commands with a definition of each command and its arguments. *Magers, 1983; Smith and Mosier, 1984*

9.32 Relevant HELP
Provide situation-specific HELP.

When users request online help, the problem is often related to the transaction in use when HELP was called. Thus, it is often desirable to automatically display the HELP screen or window associated with the current transaction when the HELP request is entered. This will often save the users from having to page and search through a HELP system for relevant guidance, perhaps never finding it. More sophisticated systems may permit pointing at an object or item, requesting HELP, and getting guidance on that specific item.

9.33 Non-destructive HELP
Requesting HELP does not cause data loss.

The computer system preserves any data that users have entered, retrieved, or modified when online assistance is requested. They also are not required to log–off the application they were using in order to access HELP. The necessity to log–off would force users to restart the whole transaction sequence. *Limanowski, 1983*

9.34 HELP In Context

Maintain context during HELP.

Users should be able to maintain the context of the task that was in progress when HELP was requested. The users may have trouble relating the guidance to the task because the task screen and the HELP screen are not present at the same time. They may also lose track of the sequence of actions they had planned when interrupted by the need to seek help. The HELP system design can often reduce the likelihood or the impact of loss of context. *Limanowski, 1983; Magers, 1983; Smith and Mosier, 1984*

Examples:

1   In a system that permits overlapping windows, a HELP window can be presented so that it only partially overlays the original display. This leaves portions of the main task in view for a frame of reference.

2   A second possibility is to use a split screen with the erroneous or the last–used portion of the original screen displayed in the top portion and the HELP screen in the bottom portion.

3   Another example approach is to provide function keys that permit the user to flip quickly back and forth between the transaction screen and the HELP screen.

9.35 Succinct HELP

Keep online guidance concise.

The text included in HELP systems should be concise. Excessive verbiage or inclusion of information that is not directly relevant to the user's tasks force the user to scan more pages, increasing the time spent away from the primary task and reducing the probability of finding useful guidance. If users cannot find the answers they seek from HELP without considerable extra effort, they may not use the HELP system at all. *Magers, 1983*

9.36 HELP Data Base
Separate HELP text from programs.

Create a file, table, or data base to contain online guidance text. Like the error message data base (see 9.23), this will simplify maintenance and revision of the text.

9.37 Training Mode
Include a training mode.

When users have the capability of modifying important data files, include a training mode to allow users to learn the system without damaging data files. A small training file containing representative data could be used in this mode in place of the actual data files.

170

Chapter Ten
Implementation of Human-Computer
Interface Guidelines

This chapter contains strategies and suggestions for incorporating human-computer interface design principles and guidelines into the overall system design process. Guidelines provide a valuable and practical tool for applying user-interface concerns in a software project. They help ensure that the resulting product will be accepted and operated productively by its users without requiring much additional skill and training.

Guidelines can also have beneficial side effects for programming productivity. The user interface consistency promoted by guidelines often permits more modular and more data-independent software design, which can reduce development costs. In addition, this systematic approach to consistent user interfaces can simplify training for programmers who are new to a project. Because consistent user interface conventions have been defined and documented, new programmers will be able to use them to master this aspect of their new job much more quickly.

Guidelines are only one of several components of an effective user interface design strategy. Although this book has focused primarily on guidelines, several other steps are critical for effective human-computer interface design. This chapter will discuss these steps along with the role of guidelines in the system development process. The recommended strategy incorporates the following components:

1   establishing the human-computer interface role in system development,

2   knowing the users,

3   defining the tasks,

4   incorporating design guidelines,

5   training software designers in human-computer interface design,

6   developing user interface software tools,

7   prototyping and user testing, and

8   designing by iterative refinement.

Each of these eight steps will be discussed in detail in the following sections.

Establishing the Human-Computer Interface Role In System Development

Human-computer interface design has begun to play a larger role in system development. Several strategies have proven to be important in ensuring that user interface concerns are incorporated into the design process. Management support, participation as a team member, and appreciation for design tradeoffs are critical to the success of a human-computer interface designer.

Several useful suggestions can be offered to the human-computer interface (HCI) designer to help ensure that user-oriented concerns receive due weighting in hardware, software, schedule, and budget tradeoffs. Perhaps at the heart of all of these suggestions is the need to establish the HCI role early as a accepted team member and contributor.

10.1 Management Support
Seek management backing for HCI plans.

The need to formally seek project management backing for human-computer interface methods and plans cannot be overstated. This support will pave the way for acceptance among designers in other specialties at the working level. When tough tradeoffs must be made later, management appreciation for user interface issues will be invaluable.

Project managers are already keenly aware of the importance of user acceptance of the systems they develop, so they typically require little convincing about the need to design for usability. They do need to be convinced, however, that a given approach to user interface design is viable for their project.

A practical set of preliminary general guidelines can serve as evidence that the human-computer interface designer is already armed with useful, believable tools to help solve the problem. Well written guidelines have a powerful intuitive appeal. Almost anyone who has used a computer system has probably cursed it for not doing some of the things that guidelines recommend.

10.2 Team Participation
HCI is an integral part of the design team.

The role of the human-computer interface designer should be as an integral member of a design team. Too often the role becomes that of intermittent consultant and advisor, or worse, that of auditor after the design has progressed so far that substantive changes are impractical. HCI involvement in the project should begin in the earliest stages, when fundamental decisions having major impact on the user interface are being made.

10.3 Design Tradeoffs
HCI personnel participate in design tradeoffs.

The human-computer interface designer must accept the necessity to make design tradeoffs and to be prepared to weigh the benefits of a given guideline against its costs.

174

It is probably obvious to the readers of this book that its guidelines vary widely in their importance to usability. Also, some guidelines may be critical in certain design situations (with specific kinds of hardware, tasks, or users), but the same guidelines may be "bells and whistles", or even irrelevant, in other situations. *Shneiderman, 1983a*

HCI designers, then, must be prepared to give and take. They must be prepared to fight for capabilities that are essential, to give up occasionally on costly capabilities that are merely niceties, and to compromise at times when the "best" way from a HCI perspective might not be the optimal way from an overall system perspective.

Knowing the Users
Knowing the users is critical to successful system design. Users must be directly involved in the design process from its earliest stages and work with designers to ensure both the functionality and the usability they need.

10.4 Direct Contact with Users
Designers work directly with users.

The designers should have direct, ongoing contact with users of existing systems or potential users of new systems before system design. Discussions and interviews with users are set up to help designers understand how users do their tasks, how the proposed system could best help them, how existing systems work, and what the strengths and weaknesses of the existing systems are. As system prototypes are developed and refined, demonstrate them to users, have the users operate them, and incorporate user feedback into subsequent iterations of the prototype. *Gould and Lewis, 1983, 1985*

10.5 User Representatives
Users are represented on the design team.

Have people who are representative of typical users of the proposed system participate directly as design team members. These users can provide valuable expertise to the project about details of user jobs that may impact system design. The user representatives, because they have been directly involved in system design, can also serve as advocates to help ensure acceptance of the system by user organizations.

Note:
This guideline does not imply that user representatives should have the power to dictate design details. Users are often too familiar with old, well-learned systems and procedures to recognize the value of some improvements. However, the opinions, experience, and job knowledge of users must be represented and respected on the design team. *Gould and Lewis, 1983*

Defining the Tasks
Design must be based on an understanding of the tasks the users will perform with the system, and the physical and sociological environment in which the system will be used. *Smith, Lafue, Schoen, and Vestal, 1984*

10.6 Function Analysis
Analyze and define systems functions.

Identify, describe, and document the functions to be performed by the system. This step is essential to establish what the system is required to do before proceeding to how it will do it. *MIL-H-46855B, 1979*

10.7 Task Analysis
Analyze user tasks.

A task analysis is a time-oriented description of the user-system interactions. It shows the sequential and simultaneous manual and intellectual activities of users, rather than just sequential operation of the equipment. Two kinds of task analysis can provide valuable, systematically derived insights to guide system design. These are:

1   analysis of users' existing tasks (without the benefit of the new or proposed system), and

2   analysis of the tasks required for operation of the proposed system. *MIL-H-46855B, 1979*

■■■ **Incorporating of Design Guidelines**
Project-specific user interface design guidelines must be developed, documented, revised, and maintained. The general guidelines presented in this book and elsewhere serve as a good starting point, but they must be made much more specific and tailored to the context and constraints of the project.

176   This section has two purposes: to discuss the value of guidelines in the design process and to suggest strategies to those who are developing guidelines tailored to the environment and constraints of their own design project.

10.8 Document Concepts
Guidelines document user interface concepts.

One valuable effect of creating human-computer interface guidelines is to formalize and document concepts and agreements among designers about the project's user interface conventions. The requirement to establish and document these conventions as guidelines leads designers through several beneficial steps:

1   In the process of establishing a mutually accepted set of conventions, many important design issues and tradeoffs will be uncovered and addressed early.

2   The impacts of proposed user interface approaches on diverse design aspects (such as user needs, programming, hardware design, maintenance, testing, manuals, access control, and user support) are often revealed, leading to more balanced, optimized tradeoffs.

3 Formalizing conventions promotes consistency in the user interface in spite of the fact that many different designers, each with different personal preferences and styles, are developing different modules or components.

10.9 Provide Visibility
Guidelines give visibility to HCI concepts.

Guidelines serve another important function by taking abstract theoretical principles and transforming them into practical rules of thumb that sound more like "common sense". This makes them clear, interesting, and usable for a much broader audience. The concepts and theories, and research from which guidelines are derived are often only accessible and interesting to specialists. *Norman, 1983*

10.10 Implementable Suggestions
Develop implementable guidelines.

If guidelines are to be useful, they must present specific, relevant design rules. Platitudes and vague advice are of little value to a designer.

A good test of this quality in a guideline is the extent to which it serves as an audit criterion. If you look at a given interface design, can you readily determine whether it meets this guideline? If not, the guideline probably needs to be stated more clearly or with more specificity.

Example:

Lacks Specificity   More Useful

"Error messages   "Error messages should show:
should be clear."   1. what error has been detected
                         2. which field contains the error
                         3. what corrective action to take."

10.11 Concrete Examples
Include concrete examples.

The situations to which specific guidelines apply are usually difficult to describe without providing a context. Often the simplest and most effective way to communicate the specific intent of a guideline and provide its context is through examples.

The example should show at least a concrete, specific example of observing the guideline. Accompanying this with a corresponding example that violates the guideline can provide a convincing and dramatic contrast. This can enhance face validity and designer acceptance of the suggestion.

10.12 Local Guidelines
Establish general guidelines and local conventions.

In a large computer system program, such as a corporate data base system, several relatively autonomous design groups often work on major subsystems within the larger system. In these situations it is important to establish general guidelines to help ensure consistency and usability at the system level, especially if the same users will access more than one of the subsystems.

General guidelines, however, usually cannot provide the level of specificity necessary to serve as detailed design conventions without unnecessarily constraining options at the subsystem level. Local design convention documents, developed individually by each of the subsystems for its own use, can provide detailed guidance that is tailored to the special needs, constraints, and users of each subsystem.

Example:
In a corporate data base system development, corporate level guidelines were first established. These guidelines contained general advice like: "Locate data that appear on every screen in the same location on each page." *Brown et al., 1980, 1983*

Subsequently, we developed local design conventions within individual projects (such as finance, material, engineering). Through discussions with the project management and representatives of each design specialty group (programming, requirements analysis, user representatives, data base design, system test, and user support) agreements and compromises were made to define very specific conventions for local implementation of the general guidelines (Brown, 1981, 1982). An example of the level of detail provided in these conventions is shown in Table 10.1, which identifies specific row and column locations for each category of standard data.

Table 10.1
Example of Specific Local Conventions

Standard Field Locations

Field	Line	Column
1 Screen ID	1	2-5
2 Type of screen	1	8-13
3 Screen title	1	16-65
4 Current Date	1	72-79
5 Data base project ID	2	8-11
6 Screen subtitle	2	16-65
7 Page number	2	69-79

(based on Brown, 1982)

10.13 Realistic Guidelines
Develop realistic guidelines.

Guidelines also need to be realistic and reflect the hardware and software constraints of the system for which they are written. A few unrealistic guidelines can cause the entire set of guidelines to lose credibility. A general book like this can make few assumptions about hardware and software constraints. If the reader applies guidelines from this book in a specific setting with known constraints, they should be tailored to be realistic within those constraints.

Example:
It is not appropriate to include guidelines about windowing for a system that will not support windowing.

10.14 Advantages for Users
Guidelines benefit users.

Applying human-computer interface guidelines in system design leads to several advantages for users. We can usually expect better user productivity through faster task performance and fewer errors. Training requirements and time lost to training can be reduced. Also, many will use a system that is easily learned, but will not have the time (or take the time) to learn a system that requires a significant training investment. User acceptance, satisfaction, and utilization of the system usually increase as a result of the usability promoted by guidelines.

Examples:
Keister and Gallaway (1983) redesigned the user interface of an existing commercial software package to make it conform to several commonly accepted human-computer interface guidelines. They then compared the data entry performance of actual users of the original and revised programs. Those using the modified programs completed tasks 25 percent faster and made 25 percent fewer errors than users of the original programs.

Burns, Warren, and Rudisill (1986) revised the formats of displays used by space shuttle astronauts and flight controllers to meet accepted human-computer interface guidelines. The revised displays not only improved the performance of novice users of the displays, but even improved the performance of astronauts and controllers who were well-trained experts on the original displays.

10.15 Advantages for Design
Guidelines also benefit design projects.

Although guidelines are primarily aimed to benefit users, several side effects also benefit design projects. One obvious benefit is that if users are more satisfied, use the system more, or buy more if it is a commercial system, the design project is viewed as successful, along with its personnel. Several more benefits are discussed in the following paragraphs.

Example:
The manager of one large project said that human-computer interface guidelines permitted him to develop the system with 20 percent fewer designers and programmers than he had expected.

10.16 Standardize Procedures
Standard procedures benefit designers.

The standardization of procedures that guidelines promote not only tends to provide users with a predictable, familiar user interface, but also provides systems analysts and programmers with a familiar, common frame of reference for developing the user interface.

10.17 Design Guidance
Guidelines simplify design.

By providing a systematic, documented framework for user interface design, guidelines can simplify many design problems. They can even head off some problems before they occur, so that no valuable design time is wasted. The guidance they offer to systems analysts and programmers is often welcomed.

10.18 Standard Modules
Guidelines facilitate programming aids.

The consistency of user interface design that guidelines foster often permit programmers to use the same programming code or modules to perform user interface functions in a wide variety of applications. This dramatically reduces the amount of unique user interface code to be developed by separating it from applications modules, rather than embedding user interface code in each module.

Example:
In one data base project, the consistency required by guidelines permitted programmers to code HELP, screen request, and error message handling software into one independent module each, rather than having to embed code to support these functions into each of over 1500 transaction programs.

10.19 No "Reinventing the Wheel"
Guidelines reduce redundant effort.

The systematic approach of documented HCI guidelines also tends to reduce the likelihood that different designers will spend time independently resolving the same user interface problem (perhaps arriving at answers that are incompatible with each other).

10.20 Training New Designers
Guidelines facilitate designer training.

A documented set of standard user interface procedures and conventions can be of immense value to programmers or systems analysts, who are new-hires or transfers to an ongoing project. General guidelines, and especially local user interface conventions documents, make effective training materials.

Training Software Designers in Human-Computer Interface Design

This section discusses another aspect of the recommended strategy for implementing good human-computer interface design into a project: the educating of software designers to understand the basic principles of HCI and their importance. The last few years have seen a general increase in awareness and concern for user-oriented issues among software professionals, so the environment is good for promoting HCI.

Systems analysts, programmers, and other design personnel often need to be sensitized to the concepts and philosophy of human-computer interface design. The benefits that can accrue to the design team as well as the users must be advertised. Human-computer interface personnel must establish their role as cooperative rather than adversarial with traditional design roles.

10.21 Sensitize Designers
Sensitize designers to HCI.

HCI designers should promote a general appreciation for user-oriented philosophy and concepts among their colleagues in project management, hardware design, and software design. The ultimate success of HCI depends upon acceptance of its goals and principles within the design project.

10.22 Standard Practice
HCI methods become standard practice.

A good measure of the success of the HCI designer in a project is the extent to which HCI-originated ideas become incorporated into standard programming concepts by project software personnel.

10.23 "It's Just Common Sense"
Successful HCI becomes common sense.

When good HCI design techniques become accepted into the body of programming common knowledge, they will be carried into future projects by the software personnel and future systems will also benefit.

10.24 Test Methods Orientation
Introduce designers to testing methods early.

Train designers in the methods and plans for pilot studies, user testing, and field evaluations. An understanding of the planned procedures for test and evaluation will help designers to place a greater emphasis on usability earlier in the design cycle. If, for instance, designers know that error frequencies will be collected, their attention to error prevention and handling will increase.

Developing User Interface Software Tools
This section discusses how human-computer interface concepts can often be supported by software tools that extract user interface functions from transaction-specific code. These tools can enhance consistency in the interface almost automatically and provide an environment where iterative design is simple. Benefits in program modularity, data independence, and development time and cost can also result.

183

Trying to promote user interface design consistency in a large software system can sometimes be a major undertaking. The system is typically broken down into a large number of modules or programs, each assigned to different programmers or teams of programmers. Each programmer has different preferences, training, and experiences in user interface design. Good user interface software tools can often establish a symbiotic relationship between human-computer interface design and programming productivity. In particular, the HCI design goal of user interface consistency facilitates use of software tools that, in turn, build in de facto consistency.

10.25 Software Tools
Provide software tools for user interfaces.

The best way to ensure that HCI principles are incorporated into system design is to build them into software tools that control the user interface. These software tools can serve as general purpose intermediaries between user interactions and modules that conduct specific transactions. Thus, user interface design does not have to be repeatedly "sold" to disparate teams of programmers, nor do the programmers have to redundantly develop program specific code to support the user interface. *Fish, Gandy, Imhoff, and Virzi, 1985*

Implementation of Human-Computer
Interface Guidelines

10.26 Application Independence
Make user interfaces program independent.

There are significant benefits in making some user interface functions independent of the applications they support:

1 Prototyping, user testing, and iterative design are facilitated by permitting global user interface changes to be made without having to modify code in every transaction. *Gould and Lewis, 1985*

2 Changes in certain user interface characteristics, such as the wording of messages or HELP text, can sometimes be made by non-programmers without changing any code. *Norman, 1983*

3 The capability for users to tailor aspects of the user interface to their preferences is also easier to provide in a system with independent user interface software. *Norman, 1983*

Example:
In a data base project the wording of HELP screens and error messages were separated from the transactions to which they referred, and stored as entries in the data base. Only their index numbers were coded into the programs which called them. This permitted non-programmers (with appropriate access authorization) to modify HELP or error message wording, without changing a line of code, through normal data base edit/entry procedures.

User support personnel were thus able to improve the wording of an error message or HELP screen that had been giving users problems. They could change the text in minutes, the revision was immediately available to users, and no software changes were required. Since the user support personnel were often the first to learn, through calls for assistance, that the messages were not clear, they were well qualified to improve the wording.

■ Prototyping and User Testing
Guidelines provide an invaluable tool for human-computer interface designers, permitting them to avoid many known design pitfalls, providing them a systematic way to promote consistency, and documenting many user-oriented design practices. Guidelines alone,

however, cannot guarantee a good user interface design. Guidelines cannot foresee all the user-specific, task-specific, or organization-specific implications that may exist and interact with almost any feature of the design.

Testing the design starting early in the development cycle can reveal flaws in concepts or assumptions about what users need, want, or find easy. These tests can start very early in system development before corrections become costly or even impossible. Paper simulations of screens, dialogues, or manuals can test users' performance, understanding, and satisfaction with the evolving system even before a single line of code has been written. As system development proceeds mockups and running prototypes can be used for continued testing.

The designers must test design features and concepts on people from the population of users for which the system is targeted. Key concepts can be tested very early in conceptual design stages using paper simulations of formats, dialogues, or messages. Subsequently, prototypes of gradually increasing scope and fidelity can be tested on users. The lessons learned at each test iteration are incorporated into the next design iteration. This approach can uncover critical flaws, unworkable designs, and unrecognized user requirements early in the design process, before years of work have been invested in a design that would have ultimately been scrapped.

10.27 User Testing
Conduct testing with actual users.

Preliminary testing can use design team members, friends, or new employees, but that does not substitute for testing users from the system's target population. Tognazzini (1985) stated the importance of testing actual users quite convincingly:

Products must be repeatedly tested on "real people." ("Real people" means the target audience: as soon as you find yourself sitting in a meeting with other computerists, all announcing what users will or will not feel/think/do, you are in trouble -- build the prototype and find out.)

10.28 Behavioral Measurement
Measure user behavior, not just opinions.

Observe and measure the performance of users actually operating the simulated or prototype system. Reviews and demonstrations alone do not require users to deal with the details of system operation firsthand, so the opportunity to collect valuable diagnostic data may be lost. Empirical data should be systematically collected, including learning time, the number and types of errors made, the time taken to complete tasks, retention, and the users' preferences and satisfaction with various aspects of the system. *Gould and Lewis, 1985; Shneiderman, 1983c*

10.29 Paper Tests
Early testing can use paper.

Long before any coding of system software has begun, early user interface concepts can be tested by providing users with paper simulations of the interface design. Simulated user manuals, system usage scenarios, paper simulations of screen formats, and paper-and-pencil tasks that simulate certain critical aspects of the user interface can be used to test and refine concepts and plans. *Gould and Lewis, 1985; Shneiderman, 1983c*

10.30 Simulation Tests
Pre-operational tests can simulate planned systems.

By simulating planned systems, more sophisticated tests can be conducted before an operational prototype is available. For example, a hidden human operator can simulate the responses that a planned, but currently nonexistent system would make.

Example:
Gould, Conti, and Hovanyecz (1982,1983) used a simulation to study user performance on an automated dictation system, or "listening typewriter", in spite of the fact that speech recognition technology did not yet allow unrestricted dictation to a computer. The experiment had users speak into a microphone. Their dictated words were subsequently displayed back to them on a CRT. Unseen by the subject, a typist in another room listened to the subject's dictation and typed the words into the computer. This testing method has been named the "Wizard of Oz" technique (Kelley, 1983; Green and Wei-Haas, 1986). Gould and his colleagues were able to make valuable conclusions about the effects of

vocabulary size and connected-word versus isolated-word speech through this simulation, even though the technology to support automatic dictation does not exist yet.

10.31 Prototype Tests
Use system prototypes for testing.

A prototype is an early version of a system that exhibits the essential features of the later operational system. Prototypes can be valuable in system development from several different perspectives:

1 they are working systems which permit testing through operational use,

2 they enhance user understanding of the system by permitting users to experience the implications of design concepts firsthand,

3 they provide a medium for identifying and refining poorly-defined user requirements,

187

4 design problems can be detected and corrected earlier in the development process and at less cost,

5 they promote an active user role in system development, user commitment to the system, and thus user acceptance of the system,

6 they promote communication between users and designers,

7 they provide real data for use in estimating the resource requirements of the operational system, such as development cost and schedule, response time, and computer capacity requirements,

8 a prototype can be a very effective marketing and demonstration tool,

9 the final prototype iteration may sometimes become the operational system, and

1 0 design by prototyping often requires less time and money than traditional approaches.

Alavi, 1984a, 1984b

■■■ Designing by Iterative Refinement

As ongoing tests with users reveal needed changes and refinements, the design must be updated. It may appear that this process will make the development cycle cost more and take longer. However, early testing and iterative design will usually speed development by detecting and remedying problems early before vast time and money resources have been expended on unworkable designs or inadequately specified requirements.

Iterative design is a critical component of the user testing and prototyping development cycle. The problems discovered in a test cycle must be addressed in a revised design, then the revised design must be tested. (Otherwise, there is no guarantee that the revised design is better than the original.)

10.32 Iterative Design

Redesign in response to user testing.

It is important that the lessons learned from testing, simulations, and prototypes be incorporated into a revised system design. Revision and retesting of the design by measuring user performance should be repeated as many times as necessary. This may seem to be an expensive and slow process, but experience in diverse systems has often shown that the prototyping, testing, and iterative design approach actually takes less time than traditional approaches. Prototypes and design iteration can help get a project going by stimulating thought, providing a concrete embodiment of design plans, and providing something tangible to show others. *Gould and Lewis, 1985; Tognazzini, 1985*

Examples:

Alavi (1984b) has shown that one project using this approach spent about 9 percent of its total man-months in the system requirements definition phase, while seven similar projects using traditional approaches averaged about 19 percent of total man-months in requirements definition.

10.33 Ongoing Feedback
Collect ongoing user feedback.

Once a system is available to users, ongoing feedback from several media is available for use in evaluating and improving the system. Potential sources of valuable feedback include:

1   an online suggestion box,

2   electronic mail messages for design and user support personnel,

3   user assistance consultants (online, telephone, or in person advisors),

4   online and paper surveys and questionnaires,

5   interviews, and

6   records of the number of occurrences of specific errors, commands, menu calls, transaction requests, and help requests.

Chapter Eleven

References

Alavi, M. An assessment of the prototyping approach to information systems development. *Communications of the ACM*, 1984(a), *27(6)*, 556-563.

Alavi, M. The evolution of information systems development approach: some field observations. *Data Base*, 1984(b), *15(3)*, 19-24.

Albert, A.F. The effect of graphic input devices on performance on a cursor positioning task. *Proceedings of the Human Factors Society - 26th Annual Meeting*, 1982, 54-58.

Barnard, P., Hammond, N., MacLean, A., and Morton, J. Learning and remembering interactive commands. *Proceedings of Human Factors in Computer Systems.* Washington, D.C. Chapter, Association for Computing Machinery, 1982, 2-7.

Bergum, B. O. and Bergum, J. E. Population stereotypes: an attempt to measure and define. *Proceedings of the Human Factors Society - 25th Annual Meeting,* 1981, 662-665.

Beringer, D.B. and Peterson, J.G. Touch input devices: training the device or the operator? *Proceedings of the Human Factors Society - 27th Annual Meeting*, 1983, 206–210.

Beringer, D.B. and Peterson, J.G. Underlying behavioral parameters of the operation of touch-input devices: biases, models, and feedback. *Human Factors,* 1985, *27(4)*, 445-458.

Black, J.B. and Moran, T.P. Learning and remembering command names. *Proceedings of Human Factors in Computer Systems.* Washington, D.C. Chapter, Association for Computing Machinery, 1982, 8-11.

Broadbent, D. E. Language and ergonomics. *Applied Ergonomics,* 1977, *8,* 15-18.

Brown, C. M. *Video displays: design and use.* Sunnyvale, CA: Lockheed Missiles and Space Company, August, 1981.

Brown, C. M. *Video display design guide.* Sunnyvale, CA: Lockheed Missiles and Space Company, June, 1982.

Brown, C. M., Brown, D. B., Burkleo, H. V., Mangelsdorf, J. E., Olsen, R. A., and Perkins, R. D. *Human factors engineering standards for information processing systems.* Sunnyvale, CA: Lockheed Missiles and Space Company, 15 June 1983.

Brown, C.M., Burkleo, H. V., Mangelsdorf, J. E., Olsen, R. A., and Williams, A. R. *Human factors engineering criteria for information processing systems.* Sunnyvale, CA: Lockheed Missiles and Space Company, 10 October 1980.

Burns, M.J., Warren, D.L., and Rudisill, M. Formatting space-related displays to optimize expert and nonexpert performance. In *Proceedings of CHI '86 Human Factors in Computing Systems* (Boston, April 13-17, 1986), Association for Computing Machinery, New York, 274-280.

Cakir, A., Hart, D.J., and Stewart, D.F.M. *Visual display terminals.* New York: Wiley, 1980.

Card, S.K., English, W.K., and Burr, B.J. Evaluation of mouse, rate–controlled isometric joystick, step keys, and text keys for text selection on a CRT. *Ergonomics,* 1978, *21*, 601–613.

Carter, R.C. Visual search and color coding. *Proceedings of the Human Factors Society - 23rd Annual Meeting,* 1979, 369-373.

Carlson, E. D. Graphics terminal requirements for the 1970s. *Computer,* August 1976.

Chapanis, A. Words, words, words. *Human Factors,* 1965, *7(1)*, 1-17.

Chapanis, A. Design of controls. In Van Cott and Kincade (Eds.) *Human engineering guide to equipment design.* U.S. Government Printing Office, 1972.

Christ, R. E. Review and analysis of color coding research for visual displays. *Human Factors,* 1975, *17*, 542-570.

Dean, M. How a computer system should talk to people. *BM Systems Journal,* 1982, *21(4)*, 424-453.

Doherty, W.J. and Kelisky, R.P. Managing VM/CMS systems for user effectiveness. *IBM Systems Journal,* 1979, *18(1),* 143-163.

Douglas, S.A. and Moran, T.P. Learning text editor semantics by analogy. In *Proceedings of CHI '83 Human Factors in Computing Systems* (Boston, December 12-15, 1983), Association for Computing Machinery, New York, 207-211.

Durrett, J. and Trezona, J. How to use color displays effectively. *Byte,* April, 1982, 50-53.

Ehrenreich, S. L. Query languages: design recommendations derived from the human factors literature. *Human Factors,* 1981, 23(6), 83-86.

Ehrenreich, S.L. Computer abbreviations: evidence and synthesis. *Human Factors,* 1985, *27(2),* 143-155.

Engel, S. E. and Granda, R. E. *Guidelines for man-display interfaces.* Poughkeepsie, NY: IBM, TR 00.2720, 1975.

Elam, P. G. Human considerations. *Computerworld,* March 31, 1980, 1-10.

Estes, W.K. Is human memory obsolete? *American Scientist,* 1980, 68, 62-69.

Fish, R.S., Gandy, K., Imhoff, D.L., and Virzi, R.A. Tool sharpening: designing a human-computer interface. *Proceedings of the Human Factors Society - 29th Annual Meeting,* 1985, 475-479.

Fitts, P. M. and Seeger, C. M. Stimulus-response compatibility: spatial characteristics of stimulus and response codes. *Journal of Experimental Psychology,* 1953, *46,* 199-210.

Foley, J. D. and Wallace, V. L. The art of natural graphic man-machine conversation. *Proceedings of the IEEE.* April, 1974, *62(4).*

Frey, P. R., Sides, W. H., Jr., Hunt, R. M., and Rouse, W. B. *Computer generated display system guide. Volume 1.* Palo Alto, CA: Electric Power Research Institute, March 1983.

Galitz, W. O. *Screen format designer's handbook.* Chicago: CNA, 1978.

Galitz, W. O. *Human factors in office systems: a review.* Chicago: CNA, May 1, 1980.

Galitz, W. O. *Handbook of screen format design.* Wellesley, MA: Q. E. D. Information Sciences, 1981.

Galitz, W. O. *Handbook of screen format design* (Second edition). Wellesley, MA: Q. E. D. Information Sciences, 1985.

Gallaway, G.R. Response times to user activities in interactive man/machine computer systems. *Proceedings of the Human Factors Society - 25th Annual Meeting,* 1981, 754-758.

Gould, J.D., Conti, J., and Hovanyecz, T. Composing letters with a simulated listening typewriter. In *Proceedings of Human Factors in Computing Systems,* (Gaithersburg, MD, March 15-17, 1982), 367-370.

Gould, J.D., Conti, J., and Hovanyecz, T. Composing letters with a simulated listening typewriter. *Communications of the ACM,* 1983, 26(4), 295-308.

Gould, J.D. and Lewis, C. Designing for usability -- key principles and what people think. In *Proceedings of CHI '83 Human Factors in Computing Systems* (Boston, December 12-15, 1983), Association for Computing Machinery, New York, 50-53.

Gould, J.D. and Lewis, C. Designing for usability: key principles and what people think. *Communications of the ACM,* 1985, *28(3),* 300-311.

Granda, R.E., Teitelbaum, R.C., and Dunlap, G.L. The effect of VDT command line location on data entry behavior. *Proceedings of the Human Factors Society - 26th Annual Meeting,* 1982, 621-624.

Green, P. and Wei-Haas, L. The rapid development of user interfaces: experience with the Wizard of Oz method. *Proceedings of the Human Factors Society - 29th Annual Meeting,* 1985, 470-474.

Grether, W.F. and Baker, C.A. Visual presentation of information. In Van Cott and Kincade (Eds.) *Human engineering guide to equipment design.* U.S. Government Printing Office, 1972.

Grudin, J. and Barnard, P. The cognitive demands of learning and representing command names for text-editing with varying structural and semantic attributes. *Human Factors*, 1984, *26*, 407-422.

Grudin, J. and Barnard, P. When does an abbreviation become a word? and related questions. In *Proceedings of CHI '85 Human Factors in Computing Systems* (San Francisco, April 14-18, 1985), Association for Computing Machinery, New York, 121-125.

Halasz, F.G.. and Moran, T.P. Mental models and problem solving in using a calculator. In *Proceedings of CHI '83 Human Factors in Computing Systems* (Boston, December 12-15, 1983), Association for Computing Machinery, New York, 212-218.

Hansen, O.K. Human factors design consideration in military: color graphic design issues in user interface design. *Proceedings of the National Computer Graphics Association*, 1984, 235-253.

Hayes, P., Ball, E., and Reddy, R. Breaking the man-machine communications barrier. *Computer*, March,1981.

Hendricks, D., Kilduff, P., Brooks, P., Marshak, R., and Doyle, B. *Human engineering guidelines for management information systems.* Aberdeen Proving Ground, MD: U. S. Army Human Engineering Laboratory, 1 November 1982.

Hinsley, D. A. and Hanes, L. F. *Human factors considerations for graphic displays.* Pittsburgh: Westinghouse Research and Development Center, June 8, 1977.

Hollingsworth, S.R. and Dray, S.M. Implications of post–stimulus cueing of response options for the design of function keyboards. *Proceedings of the Human Factors Society - 25th Annual Meeting,* 1981, 263-265.

IBM, *Human factors of workstations with display terminals.* Technical Report G320-6102-1 (Second Edition), San Jose: IBM, 1979.

IBM, *Human factors of workstations with display terminals.* Technical Report G320-6102-2 (Third Edition), San Jose: IBM, 1984.

Jones, P. F. Four principles of man-computer dialogue. *Computer-Aided Design,* 1978, 10(3), 260-265.

Keister, R.S. and Gallaway, G.R. Making software user friendly: an assessment of data entry performance. *Proceedings of the Human Factors Society - 27th Annual Meeting,* 1983, 1031-1034.

Kelley, J.F. An empirical methodology for writing user-friendly natural language computer applications. In *Proceedings of CHI '83 Human Factors in Computing Systems* (Boston, December 12-15, 1983), Association for Computing Machinery, New York, 193-195.

Krebs, M. J., Wolf, J. D., and Sandvig, J. G. *Color display design guide.* Office of Naval Research Technical Report No. ONR-CR213-136-3F, October, 1978.

Limanowski, J.J. On–line documentation systems: history and issues. *Proceedings of the Human Factors Society - 27th Annual Meeting,* 1983, 1027–1030.

Lu, C. Computer pointing devices: living with mice. *High Technology,* January 1984, 61-65.

Magers, C.S. An experimental evaluation of on–line HELP for non–programmers. In *Proceedings of CHI '83 Human Factors in Computing Systems* (Boston, December 12-15, 1983), Association for Computing Machinery, New York, 277–281.

Marcus, A. Designing the face of an interface. *SIGGRAPH '80 Conference Proceedings.* NY: Association for Computing Machinery, 1980, 207-215.

Marcus, A. Computer graphics today, tutorial 3: icon design requires clarity, consistency. *Computer Graphics Today,* November 1984a, 1(5).

Marcus, A. Corporate identity for iconic interface design: the graphic design perspective. *Interfaces in Computing,* 1984b, *2,* 365-378.

Martin, J. *Design of man-computer dialogues.* Englewood Cliffs, NJ: Prentice-Hall, 1973.

McCormick, E. J. *Human factors engineering.* New York: McGraw-Hill, 1970.

197

McCormick, E. J. *Human factors in engineering and design.* New York: McGraw-Hill, 1976.

McTyre, J.H. and Frommer, W.D. Effects of character/background color combinations on CRT character legibility. *Proceedings of the Human Factors Society - 29th Annual Meeting,* 1985, 779-781.

Michealis, P.R. Fundamentals of speech technology. *Proceedings of the Human Factors Society - 28th Annual Meeting,* 1984, 552–554.

MIL-H-46855B. *Human engineering requirements for military systems, equipment and facilities.* US Dept. of Defense, 31 January 1979.

MIL-STD-1472C. *Human engineering design criteria for military systems, equipment, and facilities.* US Dept. of Defense, 2 May 1981 (including Notice 1, 1 September 1983 and Notice 2, 10 May 1984).

Miller, R.B. *Response times in man-computer conversational transactions.* Poughkeepsie, NY: IBM, TR 00.1660-1, 1968.

Myers, B.A. The importance of percent-done progress indicators for computer-human interaction. In *Proceedings of CHI '85 Human Factors in Computing Systems* (San Francisco, April 14-18, 1985), Association for Computing Machinery, New York, 11-17.

Nakatani, L.H. and Rohrlich, J.A. Soft machines: a philosophy of user–computer interface design. In *Proceedings of CHI '83 Human Factors in Computing Systems* (Boston, December 12-15, 1983), Association for Computing Machinery, New York, 19-23.

Norman, D.A. Design principles for human-computer interfaces. In *Proceedings of CHI '83 Human Factors in Computing Systems* (Boston, December 12-15, 1983), Association for Computing Machinery, New York, 1-10.

Olsen, R.A. *Handbook for the design and use of visual display terminals.* Sunnyvale, CA: Lockheed Missiles and Space Company, November, 1981.

Pace, B.J. Color combinations and contrast reversals on visual display units. *Proceedings of the Human Factors Society - 28th Annual Meeting,* 1984, 326-330.

Paller, A., Szoka, K., and Nelson, N. *Choosing the right chart: a comprehensive guide for graphics users.* San Diego: ISSCO Graphics, 1981.

Patrick, Robert L. A checklist for system design. *Datamation,* January, 1980, 147-154.

Perlman, G. Making the right choices with menus. *Proceedings of INTERACT 84,* 1984, 291-295.

Peterson, D.E. Screen design guidelines. *Small Systems World,* February 1979.

Pew, R.W. and Rollins, A.M. *Dialog specification procedures.* Report number 3129. Cambridge, MA: Bolt Beranek and Newman, September, 1975.

Pfauth, M. and Priest, J. Person–computer interface using touch screen devices. *Proceedings of the Human Factors Society - 25th Annual Meeting,* 1981, 500-504.

Price, H.E. The allocation of functions in systems. *Human Factors,* 1985, 27, 33-46.

Ramsey, H.R. and Atwood, M.E. *Human factors in computer systems: a review of the literature.* Technical Report SAI-79-111-DEN. Englewood, CO: Science Applications, Inc., 1979.

Reinhart, W. and Marken, R. Control systems analysis of computer pointing devices. *Proceedings of the Human Factors Society - 29th Annual Meeting,* 1985, 119-121.

Rich, E. Natural–language interfaces. *Computer,* 1984, 7(9), 39–47.

Roberts, T.L. and Moran, T.P. The evaluation of text editors: methodology and empirical results. *Communications of the ACM,* 1983, 26(4), 265-283.

Robertson, P. J. *A guide to using color on alphanumeric displays.* IBM Technical Report No. G320-6296-0, June, 1980.

Rogers, W.H. and Moeller, G. Comparison of abbreviation methods. *Human Factors,* 1984, 26(1), 49-59.

Savage, R.E., Habinek, J.K., and Blackstad, N.J. An experimental evaluation of input field and cursor combinations. *Proceedings of the Human Factors Society - 26th Annual Meeting,* 1982, 629-633.

Schmid, C.F. and Schmid, S.E. *Handbook of graphical presentation.* New York: John Wiley and Sons, 1979.

Schwartz, D.R. and Howell, W.C. Optional stopping performance under graphic and numeric CRT formatting. *Human Factors,* 1985, *27(4),* 433-444.

Seibel, R. Data entry devices and procedures. In Van Cott and Kincade (Eds.) *Human engineering guide to equipment design.* U.S. Government Printing Office, 1972.

Seminara, J.L. and Eckert, S.K. *Human factors methods for nuclear control room design. Volume 4: Human factors considerations for advanced control board design.* EPRI Report NP-1118, Volume 4, Palo Alto, CA: Electric Power Research Institute, March, 1980.

Shinar, D., Stern, H.I., Bubis, G., and Ingram, D. The relative effectiveness of alternative selection strategies in menu driven computer software. *Proceedings of the Human Factors Society - 29th Annual Meeting,* 1985, 645-647.

Shneiderman, B. Human factors experiments in designing interactive systems. *Computer,* December 1979, 9-19.

Shneiderman, B. *Software psychology: human factors in computer and information systems.* Cambridge, MA: Winthrop Publishers, 1980.

Shneiderman, B. Designing computer system messages. *Communications of the ACM,* 1982a, 25(9), 610-611.

Shneiderman, B. The future of interactive systems and the emergence of direct manipulation. *Behaviour and Information Technology,* 1982b, *1(3),* 237-256.

Shneiderman, B. *Design issues and experimental results for menu selection systems.* University of Maryland Technical Report No. CS-TR-1303, CAR-TR-26, July 1983a.

Shneiderman, B. Direct manipulation: A step beyond programming languages. *Computer*, 1983b, *16(8),* 57-69.

Shneiderman, B. Human engineering management plan for interactive systems. *Proceedings of COMPCON '83*, Washington, DC, September 25-29, 1983c, 230-238.

Shneiderman, B. *Response time and display rate in human performance with computers.* University of Maryland Technical Report No. CS-TR-1302, CAR-TR-25, October 1983d.

Shneiderman, B. *Designing the user interface: strategies for effective human-computer interaction.* Reading, MA: Addison-Wesley, 1986.

Simpson, C.A., McCauley, M.E., Roland, E.F., Ruth, J.C., and Williges, B.H. System design for speech recognition and generation. *Human Factors,* 1985, *27(2),* 115-141.

Smith, D. C., Irby, C., Kimball, R., Verplank, B., and Harslem, E. Designing the Star user interface. *Byte*, April, 1982, 242-282.

Smith, R.G., Lafue, G.M.E., Schoen, E., and Vestal, S.C. Declarative task description as a user-interface structuring mechanism. *Computer*, 1984, *17(9),* 29-38.

Smith, S.L. Color coding and visual search. *Journal of Experimental Psychology,* 1962, *64,* 434-440.

Smith, S.L. Color coding and visual separability in information displays. *Journal of Applied Psychology*, 1963, *47,* 358-354.

Smith, S.L. and Aucella, A.F. *Design guidelines for the user_interface to computer based information systems.* Technical Report ESD-TR-83-122. Bedford, MA.: MITRE Corp., March, 1983.

Smith, S.L. and Goodwin, N.C. Another look at blinking displays. *Human Factors,* 1972, *14(4),* 345-347.

References

Smith, S.L. and Mosier, J.N. *Design guidelines for user–system interface software.* Technical Report ESD–TR–84-190. Bedford, MA.: MITRE Corp., September, 1984.

Stahr, L.B. Graphically speaking. *Personal Computing.* November, 1984, 104-113.

Swezey, R.W. and Davis, E.G. A case study of human factors guidelines in computer graphics. *IEEE Computer Graphics and Applications,* November, 1983, 21-30.

Teichner, W.H., Christ, R.E., and Corso, G.M. *Color research for visual displays.* Technical Report ONR-CR213-102-4F. Arlington, VA: Office of Naval Research, 1977.

Teitelbaum, R. C. and Granda, R. E. The effects of positional constancy on searching menus for information. In *Proceedings of CHI '83 Human Factors in Computing Systems* (Boston, December 12-15, 1983), Association for Computing Machinery, New York, 150-153.

Thadhani, A.J. Interactive user productivity. *IBM Systems Journal,* 1981, *20(4),* 407-423.

Tognazzini, B. *The Apple II human interface guidelines.* Cupertino, CA: Apple Computer, March 21, 1985.

Tullis, T.S. The formatting of alphanumeric displays: a review and analysis. *Human Factors,* 1983, *23,* 657-682.

Tyler, M. Touch screens: big deal or no deal? *Datamation,* 1984, 146-154.

Whiteside, J., Jones, S., Levy, P.S., and Wixon, D. User performance with command, menu, and iconic interfaces. In *Proceedings of CHI '85 Human Factors in Computing Systems* (San Francisco, April 14-18, 1985), Association for Computing Machinery, New York, 185-191.

Williams, A.R. and Olsen, R.A. *Guidelines for the design and use of electronic display systems.* Sunnyvale, CA: Lockheed Missiles and Space Company, December, 1980.

Williges, B. H. and Williges, R. C. *User considerations in computer based information systems.* Technical report CSIE-81-2, Blacksburg, VA: Virginia Polytechnic Institute and State University, September, 1981.

Woodmansee, G. Visi On's interface design. *Byte,* July, 1983, 166-182.

Wright, P. and Barnard, P. 'Just fill in this form' -- a review for designers. *Applied Ergonomics,* 1975, *6(4),* 213-220.

203

References

Chapter Twelve
Author Index

207

Chapter Thirteen
Subject Index

A

abbreviation, 52-57
    command, 130, 111
    common, 54
    consistent, 53
    conventions, 56
    decoding, 111
    encoding, 111
    labels vs. entries,111
    menu items, 101
    rules, 111
    define on screen, 55
    dictionary, 53
    encoding vs. decoding, 53, 54
    HELP explanation of, 167, 168
    length, 52
    multiple, 55
    obscure, 54
    truncation, 53
    unnecessary, 54
    when to use, 54
access, to settings, 98
acknowledgement, button, 105
acoustic
    touch sensitive device, 135
active voice, sentences, 62
affirmative statements, 62
    error messages, 164
alarms, color, 74
allocation of functions, 4-8
alphabetic data, left justify, 24
alphabetical order
    menu items, 102
alphanumeric codes, 29-31
alphanumeric keyboard
    summary, 154-155
    uses, 151
ambiguous, wording, 60
analogies, use of, 9-11
Apple, Macintosh, 10
application independence
    benefits to HCI, 184
arm support, light pen, 145
    mouse, 139
    touch device, 136

arrangement of data
    consistency, 32
    relationships, 33
arrow keys
    cursor selection, 153
    vs. mouse, 140
    vs. mouse, joystick, etc, 151
artificial intelligence
    voice entry, 147
auditory error signals
    conservative use, 160
auditory feedback
    touch device, 137

B

bar charts, changing values, 86
beeps
    auditory error signals, 160
behavioral measurement
    user testing, 186
bells, auditory error signals, 160
black, base color, 74
blank lines, for readability, 38
    to group, 38
blank screen, 95
blinking, cursor, 47
    highlighting, 46
    levels, 47-48
    rate, 48
    use sparingly, 47
blue, use of, 75, 76
boxes, highlighting, 46
    to show relationship, 33
brevity, error messages, 162
brightness highlighting, 43-45
    number of levels, 48
buttons, definition, 105
    mouse, 138
    size on touch devices, 137
    soft controls, 105
    touch selection, 136
    typical uses, 105

C

cancel, button, 105

capabilities
  online list for system, 167
capacitive
  touch sensitive device, 135
capital letters, highlighting, 46
  use of, 26
caption, column, 127
  format specifications, 124
  location, 127
  field, 127
  upper case, 26
case, in codes, 30
  upper/lower, 26
changing values, graphics for, 86
character format options
  example, 109
characters, non-printing, 98
charts, show relationships, 82
  trend displays, 84
  vs. tables, 77
check boxes, definition, 106
checklist, soft control menus, 105
choice boxes, definition, 106
  on/off control, 106
chronological order
  menu items, 102
clear icon design, 90
clutter, 37
coarse positioning
  touch device, 137
codes, alphanumeric, 29-31
  define valid, 124
  definition of, 41
  HELP explanation of, 167
  length of, 30
  meaningful, 30
  mnemonic, 30, 57
  selection , 30
coding, consistency, 57
  defined, 57
  meaningful, 57
cold temperature, color, 76
colon, input field indicator, 125
  prompt indicator, 130
color, 66-77
  adjustment, 69

alarms, 74
appropriate uses, 66-69
assigning color codes, 70-77
associations, 71
background, 73
base color, 74
blindness, 67, 71
code defined on screen, 70
cold temperature, 76
conservative use, 66-68, 72
consistency, 70
contrast, 73
conventions, 70
CRT characteristics, 66-67
display format, 69
display medium effects, 66-67
for differentiation, 76
"go" conditions, 75
graphics, 77
highlighting, 45, 68, 72
hot temperature, 74
legibility, 66
meanings, 71
meanings defined on screen, 70
monochrome compatible, 69, 77
normal conditions, 75
primary, 66
printout, 69
recommended code, 74-77
redundant coding, 69
registration, 69
reverse video, 48, 73
saturation, 75
search tasks, 68
similar colors, 72
status indicators, 68
stereotypes, 11
task relevant, 66, 72, 67
to show relationship, 33
use of blue, 75
warning conditions, 75
weak color vision, 67, 71
column, caption, 127
  headings, 35
  units, 36
  organization of data, 25

211

212

213

215

instructions, location, 33
interactive delay
    response time, 118
intermittent use
    touch device, 136
international symbols, icons, 89
interpolation, graphics, 86
invalid input, response to, 158
inverse functions
    reversible actions, 98
irreversible, actions, 112
item, wording in menus, 101
item numbers, 42
    spacing, 43
iterative design
    application independence, 184
    user testing, 188
iterative refinement, 188

J

jargon, technical, 59, 60
joystick, cursor positioning, 150
    description, 149
    keyboard integration, 150
    summary, 154-155
    uses, 150
    vs. cursor control keys, 151
jump keys, cursor selection, 153
    vs. mouse, 140
justification, headings, 35
    left, 24
    right, 28

K

keyboard, alphanumeric, 151
    cursor control keys, 151
    entering text, 151
    input device, 151
    reliance on, 134
    uses, 151
keyboard integration
    joystick, 150
keywords, commands, 115
    entry, 129

L

labeling, consistency, 35
    function keys, 143
    fields, 34
    location, 127
    meaningful, 57
    upper case, 26
layout, function keys, 143
    screen format, 31-45
leading zeros, optional, 128
learning, ease of, 13-17
left handedness
    cursor control devices, 151
left justify, 35
    alphabetic data, 24
legal values
    show in error messages, 163
legibility, color, 66
    icons, 90
    reverse video, 48
letters, lower case, 26
    upper case, 26
light pen,145-146
    arm support, 145
    defined, 145
    selectable fields, 146
    summary, 154-155
    use with soft controls, 105
    uses, 145
light pen-keyboard switching, 146
limits displays, color, 68
line-by-line dialogue
    command prompt, 132
line charts, trend display, 84
lines, to show relationship, 33
lists, 41-45
    columnar format, 25
    format, 41
    headings, 41
    numbering, 42
location, command entry, 112
    consistency, 32
    function keys, 143
    instructions, 33
    mandatory entry, 131
    optional entry, 131

location (continued)
  selection field, 40
lower case letters, use of, 26

M

MABA-MABA lists, 5,6
Macintosh, control panel, 108
macro , capability, 14
  command, 115
  definition, 115
  menu bypass, 100
magnitude control, soft dials, 107
main menu, accessible, 100
management support
  for HCI role, 173
mandatory, entry, 131
manuals, online vs. paper, 166
map displays, graphics, 86
measurement unit
  designator, 128
  familiar, 128
memorization, commands, 110
memory requirements
  placed on users, 97
mental arithmetic, graphics, 82
mental models, 8-13
mental processing, 4,5
menu, abbreviation of items, 101
  advancements, 99
  alphabetical order, 102
  as lists, 41-45
  bypass option, 14-15
  bypass techniques, 100
  caveats, 99
  chronological order, 102
  definition, 99
  experienced users, 99
  for commands, 114
  frequency order, 102
  functional order, 102
  importance order, 102
  inactive options, 102
  infrequent users, 99
  main, 100
  modern dialogues, 99
  novice users, 99

numerical order, 102
order, 102
pop-up, 99
pull-down, 99
response time, 99
response time effects, 118
selection wording, 101
sequential order, 102
shaded options, 102
soft machine, 105
touch sensitive device, 136
message, system down, 96
message data base
  error messages, 165
meters
  soft control emulation, 107
mimic displays, graphics, 82
missing entries
  error indicator, 160
misspelling, commands, 110
mnemonic, codes, 30, 42, 57
mode, indicators, 96
monochrome compatible, color, 69
mouse, 138-140
  arm support, 139
  buttons, 138
  cursor positioning, 139
  definition, 138
  direct manipulation, 139
  disadvantages, 140
  dragging, 139
  pointing device, 139
  selection, 139
  summary, 154-155
  table space required, 140
  use with soft controls, 105
  uses, 139
  vs. cursor control keys, 151
  vs. jump keys, 140
  trailing cord, 140
mouse-keyboard
  device switching, 139-140
multiple pages
  continuation, 43-45
multiple paths, 15-16
  command menus, 114

menu bypass, 100
multiple-screen transactions, 97
multi-step transaction
 error correction, 158
mutually exclusive items
 radio buttons, 107

N

noise effects, voice entry, 149
normal conditions
 color coding, 75
novice users
 benefits of menus, 99
 designing for, 13-17
number formats, 27-29
numbering items, 42
numeric keypad
 summary, 154-155
numerical order, menu items, 102

O

old error messages
 remove after correction, 160
on/off control, check boxes, 106
online, reference material, 166
 guidance, importance of, 166
 HELP, error messages, 166
optical
 touch sensitive device, 135
option, wording in menus, 101
optional, entry, 131
options, define valid, 124
 delayed-execute, 109
 displayed, 96
 exclusive choices, 109
 explicit, 96, 129
 immediate-execute, 109
 inactive, 96
 independent choices, 109
 list order, 43
order, data, 31
 menu items, 102
 options in a list, 43
 temporal, 63
organization of data, columns, 25
output fields, explained in HELP, 167

P

page, continuation, 43-45
 function keys, 143
paper form
 screen correspondence, 37
paper simulation, prototypes, 185
paper tests, user testing, 186
parameters
 configuration, 109
 re-entry of, 129
 state setting, 106
passive voice, sentences, 62, 63
pictorial displays, graphics, 80
poke points, light pen, 146
polite, error messages, 161
 wording, 63
pop-up menu, 99
 for commands, 114
population stereotypes
 defined, 12
position control, soft dials, 107
pre-operational simulation tests, 186
precise readings, graphics, 86
predicted vs. actual, graphics, 84
present tense, sentences, 63
preview mode, format check, 98
procedures, standardized, 22
program function keys, 141-144
 defined, 141
 HELP explanation of, 167
 spatial relationships, 143
 summary, 154-155
programming aids
 guidelines as, 181
progress indicators, 94-95
 count-down, 95
 counters, 95
 list operations, 95
 percent-done, 94
progressive disclosure, 16-17
prolonged use, light pen, 145
 touch device, 136
prompt character, command, 132

prompts
  clarity, 123
  distinctive, 122
  entry, 122
  format specifications, 124
  indicator character, 130
  screen location, 122
  single entry, 124
  standard location, 122
pronouns, first person, 63
  second person, 63
protected fields, 40
prototyping, 184-185
  application independence, 184
  benefits, 187
  definition, 187
  testing benefits, 187
proximity shows relationship, 33
pull-down, menu, 99
  for commands, 114
punctuation, commands, 115
  conventions, 25
  of numbers, 27-28
pushbuttons, soft controls, 105

Q
question mark
  missing entry indicator, 160

R
radio buttons, definition, 107
  mutually exclusive choices, 107
ranges
  show in error messages, 163
records of user errors, 166
red, color for alarms, 74
  color for hot, 74
  limits displays, 85
redundant coding, color, 69
reference material, online, 166
relationships among data
  techniques to show, 33
repeating keys
  cursor control keys, 152
reserved display areas, 20-21
resistance

touch sensitive device, 135

resolution, and icon design, 90
  touch device, 137
response time, 115-119
  caveats, 116
  cost of errors, 118
  dialogue considerations, 118
  direct manipulation, 118
  echo delay, 118
  file loading and saving, 119
  form-filling dialogue, 118
  interactive delay, 118
  menu dialogue, 99, 118
  recommendations, 117
  system vs. user time, 116
  task closure, 116
response to input, 158
reverse video, color, 73
  highlighting, 46
  legibility, 48
reversible actions, 17
  UNDO function, 98
revision
  previously entered data, 158
right justify, 35
  item numbers, 43
  numbers, 28

S
saturation, color, 75
scenarios, user testing, 186
screen format
  display density, 37
  paper form corresponds, 37
  standardized, 21
  paper simulations, 186
screen ID, 23
screen layout, format, 31-45
screen title, menu wording, 101
search tasks, color benefits, 68
second person, pronouns, 63
selectable fields, light pen, 146
selection, mnemonic codes, 30
  mouse, 139
  touch sensitive device, 136

220

wording in menus, 101
selection field, location, 40
self-explanatory, icon design, 90
sentence, active voice, 62, 63
    completion, 56
    main topic, 61
    present tense, 63
    short, 61
    temporal order, 63
    structure, 61-64
    structure consistency, 62
sequence
    continuation, 97
    of frequently used data, 97
sequential grouping, 32
    order of menu items, 102
settings, access to, 98
short cuts, macros, 115
similar data, consistency, 32
simulation tests
    user testing, 186
situation-specific, HELP, 168
soft control
    combined controls, 109
    conventions, 109
    examples, 104
soft dials, 107
soft machine, advantages, 104
    definition, 104
    vs. hard machine, 104
software tools
    user interface, 183
spacing, for grouping, 38
    of numbers, 27-28
specifications, format, 124
specificity, error messages, 163
speech recognition, 147-149
split screen, HELP, 169
stacking, entries, 15, 100
    menu bypass, 100
standard modules, guidelines, 181
state boxes, 106
status display
    indicator color, 68
    location consistency, 33
status information, feedback, 94

mimic displays, 82
progress indicators, 94
stereotypes, color, 71
    population, 11-12
stimulus-response compatibility, 12
stress effects, voice entry, 148
switching
    light pen-keyboard, 146
symbol, vs. icon, 87
syntax of commands
    verb-object, 113
system abort
    error protection, 165
system capabilities
    online list, 167
system data
    type-in not required, 130
system development
    HCI role, 173
system down, message, 96
system evaluation
    user feedback methods, 189
system response time, 115-119

T
TAB keys, 143
    vs. mouse, 140
table headings, 35
tables vs. graphs, 86
tailorable user interface
    application independence, 184
task analysis, 175
task definition, 175
team participation, HCI, 174
temperature, color coding, 7476
templates, voice entry, 147
terminology, 58-61
    consistent, 58
    definition, 58
    familiar, 58
    technical, 59
terms, consistent, 22
testing, user, 183-187
    introduce designers to, 183
title , screen and menu, 101

device training, 147, 148
hands or eyes busy, 148
inspection tasks, 148
noise effects, 149
numbers, 147
stress effects, 148
summary, 154-155
utterance, 147
voice templates, 147
workload, 148
voice templates, user-specific, 148

W
warning conditions, color, 75
"What you see, is what you get.", 98
white, base color, 74
windows, HELP, 169
Wizard of Oz technique, simulation
test, 186
word processing
access to settings, 98
mouse-keyboard use, 139-140
WYSIWYG, 98
wording, ambiguous, 60
consistency, 59
menu items, 101
workload, voice entry, 148
WYSIWYG, visible effects, 98

X
Xerox, Star, 10

Y
yellow, color for warnings, 75
limits displays, 85

Z
zeros, leading, 128

Chapter Fourteen
Guideline Checklist

Guidelines Checklist

Human-Computer Interface Design Guidelines
by C. Marlin "Lin" Brown
(Ablex Publishers Human-Computer Interaction Series)

Chapter 1. General Human-Computer Interface Concepts

Chapter 1 discusses general concepts and does not include specific guidelines.

Chapter 2. Designing Display Formats

2.1 Invariant Fields. Use invariant fields on each screen.

2.2 Functional Category Fields. Assign functional category fields.

2.3 Procedures. Use standard procedures.

2.4 Use of Terms. Define and use terms consistently.

2.5 Date Format. Follow the user's convention for date format.

2.6 User Conventions. Follow user's convention for common data formats.

2.7 Unique Format Identifiers. Each format has a unique ID.

2.8 Format ID Design. Assign and use format ID's methodically.

2.9 Left-Justify Alphabetic Data. Left-justify lists of alphabetic data.

2.10 Data Organization. Display lists of data in columns.

2.11 Punctuation Conventions. Use conventional punctuation.

2.12 Prose Text. Use both upper and lower case for text.

2.13 Essential Information. Display only necessary information.

2.14 Punctuation. Punctuate long numeric fields.

2.15 Right-Justify. Right-justify lists of numbers.

2.16 Decimal Numbers. Lists containing decimals use decimal alignment.

2.17 Code Structure. Letter and digits are properly grouped.

2.18 One Case. Alphabetic codes use one case.

2.19 Selection Mnemonics. Use familiar mnemonic selection codes.

2.20 Code Length. Use short codes.

2.21 Data Order. Present lists of data in useful orders.

2.22 Data Grouping Strategies. Arrange data in logical groups.

2.23 _Analogous Data._ Present similar data in similar formats.

2.24 _Location._ Use consistent data locations.

2.25 _Data Differentiation._ Make instructions distinct from data.

2.26 _Instructions Location._ Locate instructions in sequence.

2.27 _Data Relationships._ Arrange data to make relationships clear.

2.28 _Labeling._ Label each data field.

2.29 _Consistent Labels._ Position labels consistently.

2.30 _Units._ Show units used for each variable.

2.31 _Paper Form Entry._ Make entry screens correspond to report forms.

2.32 _Clutter._ Keep displays uncluttered.

2.33 _Spacing to Group._ Use blank lines to separate groups of lines.

2.34 _Display Selection Field._ Locate selection fields consistently.

2.35 _Protected Areas._ Make non-entry fields protected.

2.36 _List Heading._ A list heading defines the list.

2.37 _List Form._ List items one to a line.

2.38 _Item Enumeration._ Enumerate items with numbers, not letters.

2.39 _Option Listing._ List common options first.

2.40 _Text Descriptors._ Separate item numbers from text.

2.41 _Headings for Multiple Pages._ Display headings on each page.

2.42 _Variable-Length Listing._ Providing continuation page indicators.

2.43 _Uses of Highlighting._ Use highlighting to draw.

2.44 _Highlight Sparingly._ Use highlighting sparingly.

2.45 _Selection Highlighting._ Highlight selected items.

2.46 _Blink Coding._ Use blink coding sparingly.

2.47 _Blink Levels._ Use only two levels of blink coding.

2.48 _Blink Rate._ Use a 2 to 5 hertz blink rate.

2.49 _Brightness Highlighting._ Use only two levels of brightness coding.

2.50 _Reverse Video Highlighting._ Check legibility of reverse video.

Chapter 3. Effective Wording

3.1 _Length of Abbreviations._ Use abbreviations only if significantly shorter.

3.2 _Consistent Abbreviations._ Use only one abbreviation for a word.

4.7 <u>Color Registration.</u> Consider color registration.

4.8 <u>Definition of Code Colors.</u> Define each color code.

4.9 <u>Consistency of Color Coding.</u> Use color codes consistently.

4.10 <u>Abnormal Color Vision.</u> Coding allows for color-weak users.

4.11 <u>Color Meanings.</u> Color code reflects common color meanings.

4.12 <u>Relevant Color Codes.</u> Use task-relevant color coding.

4.13 <u>Highlight Sparingly.</u> Use color highlighting conservatively.

4.14 <u>Similar Colors.</u> Use similar colors for related data.

4.15 <u>Contrasting Colors.</u> Use contrasting colors to distinguish data.

4.16 <u>Background Color.</u> Use contrasting background colors.

4.17 <u>Reverse Video Color.</u> Use contrasting reverse video colors.

4.18 <u>Base Color</u>. use white or black as the base color.

4.19 <u>Alarms.</u> Display alarms in red.

4.20 <u>Hot</u>. use red to indicate a hot temperature.

4.21 <u>Warnings.</u> Display warnings in yellow.

4.22 <u>Normal Conditions</u>. Use green to indicate normal conditions.

4.23 <u>"Go"</u>. Use green for "go".

4.24 <u>Use of Blue.</u> Restrict saturated blue to background use.

4.25 <u>Cold.</u> Use blue to indicate cold or water.

4.26 <u>Additional Color Coding.</u> Use color for differentiation.

4.27 <u>Color Graphics.</u> Use color for graphics.

Chapter 5. Graphics

5.1 <u>Reducing Display Density.</u> Use graphics to reduce display density.

5.2 <u>Mimic Displays.</u> Use graphics to show component relationship.

5.3 <u>Displaying Relationships.</u> Use graphics to display complex relation-ships.

5.4 <u>Display of Trends.</u> Use graphic to display trends..

5.5 <u>Comparison with Projections.</u> Use graphics to display predicted vs.actual values.

5.6 <u>Display of Limits.</u> Use graphics to display actual vs. limits.

5.7 <u>Exact readings.</u> Avoid graphics for exact numeric readings.

5.8 <u>Rapidly Changing Data.</u> Use graphics for dynamic data.

5.9 Map displays. Use map displays for geographical data.

5.10 Interpolation. Use graphics for quick interpolation.

5.11 Visual Interfaces. Icons facilitate direct manipulation.

5.12 Compact Representation. Icons can save space.

5.13 International Symbols. Icons can permit international use.

5.14 Legible Icons. Design icons for legibility.

5.15 Clear Icons. Use icons that represent their meanings clearly.

5.16 Inappropriate Use of Icons. Avoid the use of confusing icons.

Chapter 6. Dialogue Design

6.1 Intermediate Feedback. Provide input acknowledge and progress indicators.

6.2 Input acknowledgement. Acknowledge successful completion.

6.3 Blank Screen. Do not leave the screen blank.

6.4 Mode Designator. Display mode indicators.

6.5 Transaction Type. Display the current transaction type.

6.6 System Entry. Explain downtime.

6.7 Explicit Options. Display available options.

6.8 Memory Requirements. Display needed information.

6.9 Sequence Continuation. Displays indicate how to continue.

6.10 Multi-screen Transactions. Place frequently used steps first.

6.11 Visible Effects. What you see is what you get.

6.12 Access to Settings. What you see is what you've got.

6.13 Reversible Actions. Provide an "undo" function.

6.14 Main Menu. Make the main menu easily accessible.

6.15 Multiple Paths. Provide menu bypass capability.

6.16 Entry Stacking. Allow type-ahead entry stacking.

6.17 Menu Wording. Use clean wording or menu selections.

6.18 Consistent Titles. Make screen titles consistent with menu wording.

6.19 Menu Order. List menu items in appropriate order.

6.20 Inactive Menu Options. Display only active menu options.

6.21 Soft Machine Menus. Consider presenting menus as soft controls.

6.22 Buttons. Use soft buttons to initiate actions.

6.23 <u>State Boxes.</u> Use state boxes to turn options on and off.

6.24 <u>Choice Boxes.</u> Use choice boxes for mutually exclusive choices.

6.25 <u>Soft Dials.</u> Use soft dials for magnitude or position controls.

6.26 <u>Combined Controls.</u> Use combinations of soft controls together.

6.27 <u>Soft Control Conventions.</u> Conventions differentiate among soft control types.

6.28 <u>Misspelling.</u> Recognize common misspellings of commands.

6.29 <u>Similar Commands.</u> Misspellings doe not cause unintended actions.

6.30 <u>Truncated Commands.</u> Allow truncation of commands.

6.31 <u>Abbreviation Rules.</u> Use consistent abbreviation rules for commands.

6.32 <u>Irreversible Commands.</u> Require confirmation of destructive commands.

6.33 <u>Command Location.</u> Use a consistent screen location for command entry.

6.34 <u>Command Consistency.</u> Use consistent command syntax, arguments and grammar.

6.35 <u>Command Syntax.</u> Use command first, object second syntax.

6.36 <u>Hierarchical Commands.</u> Use hierarchical command structures where applicable.

6.37 <u>Congruent Commands.</u> Use congruent command pairs.

6.38 <u>Distinctive Commands.</u> Choose distinctive, specific words for commands.

6.39 <u>Command Menus.</u> Consider using command menus.

6.40 <u>Command Macros.</u> Permit user-defined command sequences.

6.41 <u>Command Help.</u> Provide access to command prompts.

6.42 <u>Command Punctuation.</u> Minimize special characters in commands.

6.43 <u>Dialogue Considerations.</u> Consider response time in choosing a dialogue.

6.44 <u>Echo Delay.</u> Echo user entries instantaneously.

6.45 <u>Interactive Delay.</u> Respond to interactive request in 2 seconds.

6.46 <u>File Delay.</u> Load or save files within 10 seconds.

Chapter 7. Data Entry

7.1 <u>Distinctive Prompts.</u> Place prompts to be easily found.

7.2 <u>Location.</u> Place prompts in standard locations.

7.3 <u>Cursor Positioning.</u> Minimize cursor movement requirements.

7.4 <u>Automatic Cursor Positioning.</u> The cursor starts at the first entry field.

7.5 <u>Standardized Procedures.</u> Use standardized input procedures.

7.6 <u>Input Prompt Clarity.</u> Use clear input prompts.

7.7 <u>Single Entry Prompts.</u> Each input field has a prompt.

7.8 <u>Format Specifications.</u> Show the correct input format.

7.9 <u>Valid Options.</u> Show valid options.

7.10 <u>Default Values.</u> Show default values.

7.11 <u>Input Field Definition.</u> Show the lengths of entry fields.

7.12 <u>Finding the Cursor.</u> Field length indicators do not obscure the cursor.

7.13 <u>Locating Labels.</u> Locate caption to left of fields & above columns.

7.14 <u>Leading Zeros.</u> Do not require leading zeros.

7.15 <u>Measurement Units.</u> Display unit designators.

7.16 <u>Familiar Units.</u> Use familiar units.

7.17 <u>Reduce Keying.</u> Reduce keying requirements.

7.18 <u>Explicit Options.</u> Make available options explicit.

7.19 <u>Parameter Re-entry.</u> Avoid requirements to re-enter data.

7.20 <u>System Data.</u> Avoid type-in of data available to the system.

7.21 <u>Truncated Commands.</u> Allow truncation of commands.

7.22 <u>Prompt Character.</u> Prompt end with a colon.

7.23 <u>Use of Colons.</u> Use colons only for input prompts.

7.24 <u>Optional Entries.</u> Distinguish optional from required entries.

7.25 <u>Optional Entry Location.</u> Mandatory inputs precede optional ones.

7.26 <u>Complex Dependencies.</u> Avoid complex entry dependencies.

7.27 <u>Input Alteration.</u> Inputs can be altered.

7.28 <u>Command Prompt.</u> Use a standard character to prompt for commands.

Chapter 8. Control and Display Devices

8.1 <u>Touch Selection.</u> Use touch devices for selecting.

8.2 <u>Touch Device Use Frequency.</u> Use touch devices for intermittent inputs.

8.3 <u>Arm Support.</u> Provide arm support for touch device users.

8.4 <u>Accidental Touch Activation.</u> Design to minimize accidental activation.

8.5 <u>Touch Device Resolution.</u> Use touch for coarse positioning.

8.6 <u>Touch Button Size.</u> Use large touch sensitive areas.

8.7 <u>Touch Feedback.</u> Provide touch selection feedback.

8.8 <u>Mouse Cursor Control.</u> Use a mouse for cursor-intensive tasks.

8.9 <u>Mouse Uses.</u> Use a mouse for selecting and dragging.

8.10 <u>Mouse–Keyboard Switching.</u> Avoid frequent mouse-keyboard switches.

8.11 <u>Mouse Disadvantages.</u> Extra table space is required for a mouse.

8.12 <u>Mouse Alternative.</u> Use mouse for many targets, jump keys for few targets.

8.13 <u>Common Functions.</u> Use fixed function keys for common functions.

8.14 <u>Fixed Function Use.</u> Use fixed keys for frequent, critical functions.

8.15 <u>Active Functions.</u> Show which functions are active.

8.16 <u>Dedicated Functions.</u> Use dedicated functions critical or frequent inputs.

8.17 <u>Function Key Display.</u> Identify function keys.

8.18 <u>Consistent Functions.</u> Assign program function keys consistently.

8.19 <u>Function Key Location.</u> Consider key layout in assigning function keys.

8.20 <u>Light Pen Uses.</u> Use light pens to select, move cursor, and draw.

8.21 <u>Prolonged Light Pen Use.</u> Avoid prolonged light pen use.

8.22 <u>Light Pen Switching.</u> Avoid alternation from light pen to keyboard.

8.23 <u>Light Pen Fields.</u> Make light pen selectable fields large.

8.24 <u>Voice Command Entry.</u> Use voice to enter commands and numbers.

8.25 <u>Voice and Workload.</u> Use voice when hands or eyes are not free.

Guideline Checklist

8.26 <u>Voice Device Training.</u> Voice entry is best for predesignated users.

8.27 <u>Voice and Stress.</u> Avoid voice entry in stressful applications.

8.28 <u>Voice and Noise.</u> Avoid voice entry in noisy environments.

8.29 <u>Joystick Uses.</u> Use joystick to move cursor and track.

8.30 <u>Trackball Uses.</u> Use trackball to move cursor and to track.

8.31 <u>Handedness.</u> Cursor device design considers handedness.

8.32 <u>Alphanumeric Keyboard.</u> Use alphanumeric keyboard as general purpose entry device.

8.33 <u>Cursor Control Keys.</u> Use cursor keys for short cursor movements.

8.34 <u>Compatible Cursor Keys.</u> Key layout is compatible with movement.

8.35 <u>Repeating Keys.</u> Cursor keys repeat when held down.

8.36 <u>Faster Cursor Keys.</u> Provide double speed cursor mode.

8.37 <u>Jump Keys.</u> Arrow keys can be used as jump keys.

8.38 <u>Numeric Keypad.</u> Use numeric keypads for massed entry of numbers.

Chapter 9. Error Messages and Online Assistance

9.1 <u>Program Response.</u> Provide a response to every input.

9.2 <u>Error Recovery.</u> Input remains after error.

9.3 <u>Multi-step Transaction Errors</u>. Allow correction at the point of first error.

9.4 <u>Error Message Display</u>. Display error messages on entry screen.

9.5 <u>Highlight Errors</u>. Highlight fields in error.

9.6 <u>Missing Entries</u>. Show fields requiring missing data.

9.7 <u>Cursor Positioning</u>. Position cursor at first error.

9.8 <u>Old Messages</u>. Remove error message after correction.

9.9 <u>Auditory Error Signals</u>. Use auditory signals conservatively.

9.10 <u>Useful Error Messages</u>. Make error message instructive.

9.11 <u>Polite Phrasing</u>. Make error messages polite.

9.12 <u>Brief Messages</u>. Make error message brief.

9.13 <u>Message Content</u>. Make error message appropriate to users.

9.14 <u>Consistent Messages</u>. Use consistent error messages.

9.15 <u>Specific Messages</u>. Make error messages specific.

9.16 Directive Messages. Use directive error messages.

9.17 Show Ranges. Show valid ranges and values in error messages.

9.18 Affirmative Messages. Make error messages affirmative.

9.19 Positive Tone. Avoid harsh, condemning words in messages.

9.20 Error Help Function. Provide levels of help.

9.21 System Abort. Keep user errors from aborting a session.

9.22 System Protection. Keep user errors from destroying data.

9.23 Message Data Base. Separate message text from programs.

9.24 Error Records. Provide for recording of user errors.

9.25 Error Documentation. Document user messages.

9.26 Online Assistance. Provide online reference material.

9.27 Online Access. Provide online system information.

9.28 HELP Function. Provide a HELP function.

9.29 HELP Contents. HELP explains screens, fields, codes, and messages.

9.30 List of Abbreviations. Provide a list of abbreviations.

9.31 List of Commands. Provide an online command glossary.

9.32 Relevant HELP. Provide situation-specific HELP.

9.33 Non-destructive HELP. Requesting HELP does not cause data loss.

9.34 HELP in Context. Maintain context during HELP.

9.35 Succinct HELP. Keep online guidance concise.

9.36 HELP Data Base. Separate HELP text from programs.

9.37 Training Mode. Include a training mode.

Chapter 10. Implementation of Human-Computer Interface Guidelines

10.1 Management Support. Seek Management backing for HCI plans.

10.2 Team Participation. HCI is an integral part of the design team.

10.3 Design Tradeoffs. HCI personnel participate in design tradeoffs.

10.4 Direct Contact with Users. Designers work directly with users.

10.5 User Representatives. Users are represented on the design team.

10.6 Function Analysis. Analyze and define system functions.

10.7 Task Analysis. Analyze user tasks.

10.8 <u>Document Concepts.</u> Guidelines document user interface concepts.

10.9 <u>Provide Visibility.</u> Guidelines give visibility to HCI concepts.

10.10 <u>Implementable Suggestions.</u> Develop implementable guidelines.

10.11 <u>Concrete Examples.</u> Include concrete examples.

10.12 <u>Local Guidelines.</u> Establish general guidelines and local conventions.

10.13 <u>Realistic Guidelines.</u> Develop realistic guidelines.

10.14 <u>Advantages for Users.</u> Guidelines benefit user's.

10.15 <u>Advantages for Design.</u> Guidelines also benefit design projects.

10.16 <u>Standardize Procedures.</u> Standard procedures benefit designers.

10.17 <u>Design Guidance.</u> Guidelines simplify design.

10.18 <u>Standard Modules.</u> Guidelines facilitate programming aids.

10.19 <u>No "Reinventing the Wheel".</u> Guidelines reduce redundant effort.

10.20 <u>Training New Designers.</u> Guidelines facilitate designer training.

10.21 <u>Sensitize Designers.</u> Sensitize designers to HCI.

10.22 <u>Standard Practice.</u> HCI methods become standard practice.

10.23 <u>"It's Just Common Sense".</u> Successful HCI becomes "common sense".

10.24 <u>Test Methods Orientation.</u> Introduce designers to testing methods early.

10.25 <u>Software Tools.</u> Provide software tools for user interfaces.

10.26 <u>Application Independence.</u> Make user interfaces program independent.

10.27 <u>User Testing.</u> Conduct testing with actual users.

10.28 <u>Behavioral Measurement.</u> Measure user behavior, not just opinions.

10.29 <u>Paper Tests.</u> Early testing can use paper.

10.30 <u>Simulation Tests.</u> Pre-operational tests can simulate planned systems.

10.31 <u>Prototype Tests.</u> Use system prototypes for testing.

10.32 <u>Iterative Design.</u> Redesign in response to user testing.

10.33 <u>Ongoing Feedback.</u> Collect ongoing user feedback.